Practice Tests

for

Berk

Development Through the Lifespan
Second Edition

Prepared by

Gabrielle F. Principe
Cornell University

Naomi Tyler
Vanderbilt University

Allyn and Bacon
Boston   London   Toronto   Sydney   Tokyo   Singapore

Preface

These practice tests were prepared to accompany *Development Through the Lifespan, Second Edition,* by Laura E. Berk. They are designed to help you prepare to take multiple-choice tests in your human development course by practicing with tests similar to those your instructor might give.

At the back of this booklet are answers to all of the questions, each with a detailed explanation of the correct answer and the page number in the textbook where the material is covered.

The tests can be used in different ways. You might use them when you are in the middle of studying, as a way of identifying your areas of weakness to help guide the rest of your study session. Alternatively, you might use them when you believe you have finished studying, as a reality check to see whether you are really prepared for a test.

If you get a question wrong, open your book to the page indicated in the answer key, reread the section, and make sure you truly understand why the answer given is the right one. If you are still unsure, ask your instructor to go over it with you.

Chapter 1: Practice Test

1.1   Theories differ from opinions primarily in that theories are
      A.   unaffected by a society's beliefs.
      B.   accepted by more people than opinions.
      C.   stated in numerical or statistical form.
      D.   verifiable by scientific methods.

1.2   A psychologist who believes that there are many courses of development would most likely emphasize __________ in his or her research.
      A.   differences in the context in which development occurs
      B.   the nature-nurture controversy
      C.   discontinuous development
      D.   qualitative changes

1.3   Which of these is an important assumption of the lifespan perspective on development?
      A.   Development refers to a process of steadily improving and expanding abilities.
      B.   Events that occur during infancy and early childhood have the strongest impact on the life course.
      C.   Development is affected by a blend of biological, psychological, and social forces.
      D.   Individual development becomes more plastic with age.

1.4   Lifespan researchers emphasize that
      A.   development is highly plastic at all ages.
      B.   development consists mainly of continuous change.
      C.   nonnormative influences hinder the multidirectionality of development.
      D.   events that occur during infancy and childhood have a greater impact on the course of development than do those that take place during adulthood.

1.5   In medieval Europe,
      A.   parents believed that they could mold their children any way they wished, through instruction, example, and rewards.
      B.   children were viewed as noble savages, born with an innate plan for orderly, healthy development.
      C.   childhood was not viewed as a distinct period of development.
      D.   harsh, restrictive parenting practices were recommended as means for taming children.

1.6   Charles Darwin is considered the forefather of scientific child study because
       A. he discovered that human prenatal growth differs markedly from that of
          other species.
       B. he constructed the first theory of human development.
       C. he was the first to conduct experiments on children.
       D. his theory prompted other researchers to study children and their
          development directly.

1.7   A developmental perspective that emphasizes the resolution of conflict between
       biological drives and social expectations is known as the ___________ approach.
       A. social learning theory
       B. ecological systems
       C. psychoanalytic
       D. sociocultural

1.8   According to the behavioristic approach, the proper focus of the study of
       psychology should be
       A. unconscious impulses and drives.
       B. observable stimuli and responses.
       C. adaptive evolutionary behavior patterns.
       D. each person's unique inner experience.

1.9   One similarity between Piaget's theory and the information-processing
       perspectives is that they both emphasize
       A. children as playing an active role in their own development.
       B. cognitive development as continuous.
       C. stimulus-response associations.
       D. the importance of equilibration in producing development.

1.10   Unlike Piaget, Vygotsky
       A. emphasized discontinuous change.
       B. focused on development throughout the lifespan.
       C. emphasized the role of bidirectional influences in development.
       D. viewed development as dependent on direct teaching by adults.

1.11   Before Bronfenbrenner's theory, most researchers viewed the environment
       A. as the primary force of development.
       B. as limited to events and conditions immediately surrounding the child.
       C. in terms of reinforcements and punishments.
       D. as less important than the influence of heredity.

1.12   An important strength of the naturalistic observation method of research is that
      A.   it gives all children an equal opportunity to participate.
      B.   the conditions of the observations can be well controlled.
      C.   it produces objective, statistically reliable data.
      D.   the observations will apply to the children's everyday lives.

1.13   Ethnographers strive to minimize their influence on the culture that they are observing by
      A.   employing rigorous experimental procedures.
      B.   minimizing the time spent with the cultural community.
      C.   relying on unobtrusive techniques, such as surveillance cameras and one-way mirrors.
      D.   becoming part of the cultural community.

1.14   The inability to infer cause and effect is the major limitation of
      A.   field experiments.
      B.   laboratory experiments.
      C.   correlational designs.
      D.   longitudinal designs.

1.15   Cause-and-effect inferences can be made in experiments because
      A.   the independent variable varies randomly throughout the experiment.
      B.   an experimenter holds the dependent variable constant throughout an experiment.
      C.   participants in all treatment conditions are treated exactly alike except for the independent variable.
      D.   participants are systematically assigned to experimental conditions.

1.16   One way to randomly assign participants to experimental conditions would be to
      A.   flip a coin.
      B.   assign participants to experimental groups in the order that they show up for an experiment.
      C.   let parents choose in which experimental group they would like their children to participate.
      D.   let children choose in which experimental group they would like to participate.

1.17   Complementing a ___________ with a ___________ is a good thing for a researcher to do because laboratory findings may not always apply to everyday situations.
      A.   natural experiment; naturalistic observation
      B.   field experiment; natural experiment
      C.   structured observation; naturalistic observation
      D.   laboratory experiment; field experiment

1.18   Which of the following is NOT a concern in longitudinal research?
      A.   age-graded influences
      B.   practice effects
      C.   participants who drop out or move away
      D.   cohort effects

1.19   One important disadvantage of cross-sectional studies is that
      A.   a large number of participants often drop out.
      B.   they take more time and effort than longitudinal studies.
      C.   being in the study changes the participants' behavior.
      D.   they do not provide information about individual development.

1.20   Under what conditions is it considered acceptable to use deception in research
with children?
      A.   If the parents give their permission.
      B.   Only when the children are older than 7.
      C.   If the researcher can demonstrate to institutional committees that it is
necessary.
      D.   Never; deception is always forbidden with children.

Chapter 2: Practice Test

2.1　Human chromosomes
  A. store and transmit genetic information.
  B. come in 46 matching pairs.
  C. always come in XY pairs.
  D. are inherited from the mother only.

2.2　__________ refers to the duplication process of body cells, whereas __________ refers to the process of cell division through which gametes are formed.
  A. mitosis; meiosis
  B. mutation; mitosis
  C. meiosis; mitosis
  D. meiosis; mutation

2.3　A gamete contains _____ chromosomes, whereas a zygote is made up of _____ chromosomes.
  A. 23; 23
  B. 46; 23
  C. 46; 46
  D. 23; 46

2.4　A person whose 23rd pair of chromosomes is XY
  A. has Turner syndrome.
  B. has Down syndrome.
  C. has PKU.
  D. is male.

2.5　__________ twins are created when two different eggs are fertilized; whereas __________ twins are formed when a zygote separates into two clusters of cells.
  A. Monozygotic; dizygotic
  B. Homozygotic; heterozygotic
  C. Dominant; recessive
  D. Fraternal; identical

2.6　__________, __________, and __________ are examples of dominant homozygous, recessive homozygous, and dominant heterozygous traits, respectively.
  A. Dd; dd; DD
  B. dd; Dd; DD
  C. dd; DD; Dd
  D. DD; dd; Dd

2.7 The case of PKU demonstrates that
  A. serious inherited disorders are more often due to dominant than recessive genes.
  B. most inherited disabilities and disorders are untreatable.
  C. even if we know the genetic make up of the parents, it is difficult to predict the likelihood that children in a family will display a disorder.
  D. changes in the environment can alter the extent to which an inherited disorder influences a person's well-being.

2.8 When a harmful gene is carried on the X chromosome,
  A. females are more likely to be affected because they have two X chromosomes.
  B. males and females have an equal chance of inheriting the disorder.
  C. males are more likely to be affected because their sex chromosomes do not match.
  D. males are less likely to be affected because any recessive gene on the X has a good chance of being suppressed by a dominant gene on the Y.

2.9 Continuously varying traits, such as height, musical ability, or intelligence, are most likely determined by _______ inheritance.
  A. polygenic
  B. X-linked
  C. dominant-recessive
  D. codominant

2.10 Which of the following is true regarding chromosomal abnormalities?
  A. Abnormalities of the sex chromosomes are more severe than are most disorders of the autosomes.
  B. The most common chromosomal abnormalities involve the absence of the Y chromosome in boys or an extra X chromosome in girls.
  C. Verbal difficulties are common among girls with triple X syndrome and boys with Klinefelter syndrome.
  D. Most abnormalities of the sex chromosomes can be detected before birth using ultrasound.

2.11 Except for _________ and _________, prenatal diagnosis should not be used routinely, since other methods have some chance of injuring the fetus.
  A. ultrasound; amniocentesis
  B. maternal blood analysis; ultrasound
  C. fetoscopy; chorionic villus sampling
  D. amniocentesis; maternal blood analysis

2.12   According to the ecological systems theory, the behaviors of each family member
       affect those of others. This represents the concept of ___________ influences.
       A.   predetermined
       B.   learned
       C.   bidirectional
       D.   universal

2.13   Which of the following statements regarding poverty in the United States is true?
       A.   Most homeless families consist of women with elementary- and middle-
            school age children.
       B.   The child poverty rate is higher than that of any age group.
       C.   Over half of all children live under the poverty line.
       D.   More children than adults are homeless.

2.14   Connections between settings that influence children's lives are most common in
       A.   large urban areas.
       B.   suburbs.
       C.   low-income neighborhoods.
       D.   small towns.

2.15   Public policies safeguarding children and youth ___________ in the United States
       than in other Western industrialized nations.
       A.   have preceded those
       B.   have been more protective
       C.   have been more successful
       D.   have been slower to emerge

2.16   Which of the following countries has the highest rate of low-birth-weight
       newborns?
       A.   the United States
       B.   Kuwait
       C.   Egypt
       D.   Romania

2.17   A concordance rate of 75 percent indicates that
       A.   one-quarter of the variation in the trait can be explained by individual
            differences in environmental factors.
       B.   if one twin has the trait, the other one will have it three-quarters of the
            time.
       C.   three-quarters of the variation in the trait is due to genetic factors.
       D.   the probability that each child will have the trait is 75 percent.

2.18   Questions about the usefulness of heritability estimates and concordance rates
       have been raised for all of the following reasons EXCEPT
       A.   These statistics provide no precise information about how the traits
            develop.
       B.   These statistics refer only to the unique range of genetic and
            environmental influences in the particular population studied.
       C.   The accuracy of these statistics depends on the extent to which the twin
            pairs they are computed on reflect genetic and environmental variation in
            the population.
       D.   These statistics provide no information on the extent to which individual
            differences are due to environmental factors.

2.19   If a behavior is strongly canalized, then
       A.   it is relatively unaffected by genetic influences.
       B.   it is highly responsive to environmental factors.
       C.   only powerful environmental forces can change it.
       D.   only extreme genetic factors can modify it.

2.20   A study showed that the greater the genetic similarity between pairs of
       adolescents, the more alike they were on many aspects of child rearing. This
       finding provides support for the concept of
       A.   genetic-environmental correlation.
       B.   concordance rates.
       C.   range of reaction.
       D.   canalization.

Chapter 3: Practice Test

3.1   Which of the following has NOT occurred by the end of the period of the zygote?
- A. implantation
- B. the ectoderm begins to form the neural tube
- C. villi begin to emerge from the chorion
- D. the amnion encloses the blastocyst in amniotic fluid

3.2   The age at which a fetus can first survive, if born early, is sometime between
- A. 18 and 22 weeks
- B. 22 and 26 weeks
- C. 26 and 30 weeks
- D. 30 and 34 weeks

3.3   The period of the ___________ is the time when serious defects from teratogens are most like to occur because ___________ this time.
- A. fetus; birth takes place soon after
- B. zygote; implantation occurs during
- C. fetus; the prenatal organism is developing most rapidly during
- D. embryo; the foundations for all body parts are laid down during

3.4   Smoking during pregnancy
- A. inhibits neural cell duplication and interfers with the transfer of nutrients to the fetus.
- B. interferes with the transfer of nutrients to the fetus and draws away oxygen that the fetus needs for cell growth.
- C. causes the placenta to grow abnormally and raises the concentration of carbon monoxide in the bloodstreams of both mother and fetus.
- D. interferes with brain development and draws away oxygen that the fetus needs for cell growth.

3.5   Which of the following is NOT true regarding alcohol use during pregnancy?
- A. Even when provided with enriched diets, FAS babies fail to catch up in physical size during infancy and childhood.
- B. Mothers of FAE infants typically drink more than those of FAS infants.
- C. Mental impairment in children whose mother drank heavily during pregnancy is permanent.
- D. Alcohol in small quantities, such as 2 ounces a day taken very early in pregnancy, does not have negative effects.

3.6   Folic acid supplementation around the time of conception reduces the incidence of
___________ and adequate folate intake taken during the last 10 weeks of
pregnancy reduces the risk of ___________.
   A.   maternal high blood pressure; premature birth
   B.   genetic disorders; breech birth
   C.   neural tube defects; low birth weight
   D.   genetic disorders; premature birth

3.7   Severe emotional stress during pregnancy
   A.   interferes with brain development, resulting in structural damage and
        abnormalities in brain functioning.
   B.   causes the placenta to grow abnormally, reducing the transfer of
        nutrients, so the fetus gains weight poorly.
   C.   raises the concentration of carbon monoxide in the bloodstreams in both
        mother and fetus, displacing oxygen from red blood cells.
   D.   reduces blood flow to the uterus, and as a result, the fetus receives less
        oxygen and nutrients.

3.8   Woman who receive late or no prenatal care
   A.   are more likely than those who receive adequate prenatal care to have
        low-birth-weight infants or infants who die before birth or during the first
        year of life.
   B.   are no more likely than those who received adequate prenatal care to
        experience birth complications.
   C.   are not more likely than those who receive adequate prenatal care to
        engage in high-risk behaviors, such as smoking and drug use.
   D.   make up less than 15 percent of pregnant woman in the United States.

3.9   Which of these occurs during the third stage of labor?
   A.   The mother feels a natural urge to push.
   B.   The baby is born.
   C.   The cervix gradually dilates.
   D.   The placenta is delivered.

3.10   High levels of stress hormones produced by infants during childbirth
   A.   can lead to anoxia, or inadequate oxygen supply, during delivery.
   B.   prepare the baby to breathe effectively by causing the lungs to absorb
        excess liquid and by expanding the bronchial tubes.
   C.   lead to irritability and digestive disturbances in newborns.
   D.   cause an infant's heart rate and activity level to increase to dangerously
        high levels during childbirth.

3.11 An Apgar ___________ indicates that the infant is in good physical condition.
    A. between 4 and 6
    B. of 3 or below
    C. between 7 and 10
    D. of 10 or better

3.12 Which of the following is true concerning home delivery?
    A. Home delivery is unsafe for all women and their babies.
    B. The rate of infant death for home deliveries is high even if the attendants are well-trained and prepared to handle emergencies.
    C. Home delivery is safe only for healthy women who are assisted by a well-trained doctor or midwife.
    D. Home delivery is safe even if the baby is in a breech position.

3.13 Fetal monitors
    A. measure the baby's blood oxygen levels during labor.
    B. have saved the lives of many high-risk babies.
    C. are linked to a decreased rate of cesarean deliveries.
    D. reduce the rate of infant brain damage and death in all pregnancies.

3.14 Which country has the highest rate of cesarean delivery in the world?
    A. China
    B. Sweden
    C. Japan
    D. the United States

3.15 Which of the following is NOT true regarding low-birth-weight babies?
    A. Small-for-date infants are more likely than preterm infants to die, catch infections, and show evidence of brain damage during the first year.
    B. Both small-for-date and preterm infants probably experienced inadequate nutrition before birth.
    C. Although low birth weight, a preterm infant's weight may be appropriate for the amount of time she spent in the uterus.
    D. Small-for-date infants are full term.

3.16 Pediatricians test newborn reflexes because
    A. reflexes that persist beyond the point in development when they should normally disappear indicate that a newborn is receiving inadequate physical stimulation.
    B. the persistence of these reflexes throughout the first year of life indicates normal development.
    C. overly rigid or exaggerated reflexes indicate that a newborn is receiving inadequate nutrition.
    D. weak or absent reflexes can signal brain damage.

3.17 Breathing is even in which of the following two infant states of arousal?
      A. regular sleep and irregular sleep
      B. drowsiness and regular sleep
      C. quiet alertness and regular sleep
      D. drowsiness and quiet alertness

3.18 Which of the following is NOT true concerning infant sleep?
      A. Children and adults spend more time in REM sleep than do infants.
      B. During REM sleep, electrical brain wave activity is remarkably similar to that of the waking state.
      C. Rapid eye movement protects the health of the eye during sleep.
      D. Disturbed REM-NREM sleep cycles are often present in infants who are brain-damaged.

3.19 Which smell do bottle-fed infants prefer?
      A. any lactating woman
      B. their familiar formula
      C. a nonlactating woman
      D. any formula

3.20 "Recovery curves" on Brazelton's Neonatal Behavioral Assessment Scale (NBAS) can be used to predict
      A. whether a parent has adequate parenting skills.
      B. the child's intelligence during the preschool years.
      C. mother-infant bonding.
      D. when an infant is going to need special medical intervention.

Chapter 4: Practice Test

4.1   The skeletal age of ___________ tends to be ahead of that of ___________,
        amounting to a sex difference of about ___________ at birth.
        A.   boys; girls; 1 to 2 weeks
        B.   girls; boys; 1 to 2 weeks
        C.   boys; girls; 4 to 6 weeks
        D.   girls; boys; 4 to 6 weeks

4.2   In the prenatal period, the ___________ develop(s) more rapidly than the
        ___________.
        A.   head; lower part of the body
        B.   hands and feet; arms and legs
        C.   arms and legs; head, chest, and trunk
        D.   head, arms, and legs; chest and trunk

4.3   Synaptic pruning is the process by which
        A.   new synapses are formed as the result of stimulation by input from the
            surrounding environment.
        B.   seldom-used neurons die during the peak period of synaptic growth in
            any brain area.
        C.   neural fibers become myelinated as a result of stimulation of the brain.
        D.   seldom-stimulated neurons are returned to an uncommitted state so they
            can support the development of future skills.

4.4   Multiplication of ___________ are responsible for the dramatic increase in brain
        size during the first 2 years.
        A.   glial cells
        B.   synapses
        C.   neurons
        D.   axons

4.5   Once the two hemispheres ___________, the cortex ___________.
        A.   lateralize; loses unneeded synapses
        B.   myelinize; is no longer highly plastic
        C.   lateralize; is no longer highly plastic
        D.   myelinize; loses unneeded synapses

4.6　Research shows that early learning centers in which infants are trained with letter and number flashcards

  A. produce children who learn to read and write earlier than their agemates.

  B. produce toddlers who show improvements in intelligence and achievement motivation for only a few years.

  C. may threaten infants' interest in learning and produce responses much like those of stimulus-deprived infants.

  D. often produce children who are classified as gifted during the elementary school years.

4.7　Breast-fed babies

  A. in poverty-stricken regions of the world are more likely than bottle-fed babies to be malnourished.

  B. in industrialized nations develop stronger mother-baby relationships than do bottle-fed babies.

  C. are more likely than bottle-fed babies to be underweight.

  D. have far fewer respiratory and intestinal illnesses and allergic reactions than do bottle-fed infants.

4.8　A longitudinal study of marasmic children revealed that

  A. an improved diet leads to some catch-up growth in height, but little improvement in head size.

  B. marasmus strikes only in developing countries.

  C. once marasmic children are put on an improved diet, they soon catch up to agemates in terms of cognitive development.

  D. these children show no organic cause for their failure to grow.

4.9　__________ is a growth disorder usually present by 18 months that is caused by lack of affection and stimulation.

  A. Nonorganic failure to thrive

  B. Deprivation dwarfism

  C. Kwashiorkor

  D. Marasmus

4.10　Classical conditioning

  A. helps infants anticipate what is about to happen next, making the environment more orderly and predictable.

  B. in infancy is a precursor of voluntary behavior.

  C. allows infants to manipulate the behavior of their caretakers.

  D. often interferes with the elicitation of newborn reflexes.

4.11   When baby Sam sees his mother he gazes into her eyes and smiles widely. Sam's
       mother looks and smiles back, and then Sam looks and smiles again. This is an
       example of
           A.   extinction.
           B.   habituation.
           C.   operant conditioning.
           D.   classical conditioning.

4.12   Which of these answers makes the following statement NOT true? A baby who
       habituates to a visual pattern and then dishabituates to a new one
           A.   prefers the first stimulus.
           B.   remembers the first stimulus.
           C.   no longer responds to the first stimulus.
           D.   regards the second stimulus as new and different from the first stimulus.

4.13   Which of the following is NOT supported by research on newborn imitation?
           A.   Through imitation, adults can get babies to express desirable behavior.
           B.   Newborn imitation reflects an automatic response to particular stimuli.
           C.   Through imitation, infants notice similarities between their own actions
                and those of others.
           D.   Using imitation, newborns begin to get to know people by sharing
                behavioral states with them.

4.14   Infants gain motor control of the head, trunk, and arms before coordination of the
       hands and fingers. This is an example of the ___________ trend.
           A.   anteriorposterior
           B.   proximodistal
           C.   cephalocaudal
           D.   medialateral

4.15   Parents who compare their children's motor development with standard charts
       such as the one in the textbook should keep in mind that
           A.   there are large individual differences in the sequence of motor
                development.
           B.   typically developing children develop new motor skills at generally the
                same rate.
           C.   many motor skills are often delayed by months in normally developing
                children.
           D.   there are large individual differences in the rate of motor progress.

4.16   Among the Kipsigis of Kenya, infants are seated in holes dug in the ground and
       rolled blankets are used to keep them upright. These infants tend to
          A.   be seriously delayed in crawling, standing, and stepping.
          B.   scoot in a sitting position rather than crawl on their hands and knees.
          C.   develop the ability to walk alone much later than North American babies.
          D.   hold their heads up and sit alone considerably earlier than North
               American infants.

4.17   Research on fine motor development in infancy shows that around 3 months of
       age, infants can
          A.   reach just as effectively for a sounding object in the dark as for an object
               in the light.
          B.   obtain a moving object that changes direction.
          C.   reach for objects with one arm, rather than extending both.
          D.   use the thumb and index finger to grasp objects.

4.18   Which of the following visual stimuli would a newborn be MOST likely to prefer?
          A.   a photograph of her mother
          B.   a black-and-white drawing of a human face
          C.   a photograph of a human face
          D.   a black-and-white checkerboard with many squares

4.19   Research suggests that intermodal perception
          A.   is present at birth.
          B.   is the direct result of intermodal experience with the environment.
          C.   appears during the first month of life.
          D.   emerges as the result of independent locomotion.

4.20   According to differentiation theory, the tendency to search for __________ in the
       surrounding environment becomes more fine-tuned with age.
          A.   changing relationships between features
          B.   categories of objects and events
          C.   opportunities for experimentation
          D.   order and consistency

Chapter 5: Practice Test

5.1   Which of the following is NOT true about schemes?
- A. Children have a natural tendency to exercise their schemes repeatedly.
- B. Schemes change through adaptation and organization.
- C. The disappearance of schemes marks the transition from sensorimotor to preoperational thought.
- D. Schemes are built through direct interaction with the environment.

5.2   When children are in a state of disequilibrium
- A. they shift away from accommodation toward assimilation.
- B. they realize that new information does not match their current schemes.
- C. they are likely to construct inefficient schemes.
- D. their existing schemes are not likely to change very much.

5.3   Baby Christopher, who is in his crib, accidentally kicks the mobile hanging over him and then watches the effect with pleasure. Later, he tries to kick the mobile again and again. According to Piaget, Christopher is using a
- A. reflexive circular reaction.
- B. primary circular reaction.
- C. secondary circular reaction.
- D. tertiary circular reaction.

5.4   When infants begin to combine secondary circular reactions into more complex action sequences, two landmark cognitive changes take place. These are __________ and __________.
- A. deferred imitation; animistic thinking
- B. conservation; centration
- C. adaptation; organization
- D. intentional behavior; object permanence

5.5   Habituation-dishabituation research has revealed that 3 1/2-month-olds who do not search for hidden objects may simply lack
- A. the separate schemes to retrieve hidden objects.
- B. the ability to engage in goal-directed behavior.
- C. an appreciation for physical causality.
- D. the ability to grasp the idea of object permanence.

5.6   Which of the following is a major valid criticism of Piaget's conceptualization of development during the sensorimotor stage?
       A.   Motor activity does not facilitate the development of infants' representational capacities.
       B.   Infants appear to have the ability to form mental representations at birth, a capacity Piaget assumed was the culmination of the sensorimotor stage.
       C.   Constructive interaction between the child and the environment is not a major force behind sensorimotor development.
       D.   Infants comprehend a great deal about the world before they are capable of the motor behaviors Piaget assumed were responsible for those understandings.

5.7   Which of the following statements is supported by information-processing research?
       A.   Developmental changes in the structure of the mental system account for age differences in information-processing capacity.
       B.   Information-processing capacity remains relatively stable throughout childhood and adulthood.
       C.   Most age-related gains in processing capacity are due to developmental differences in strategy use.
       D.   Developmental increases in processing capacity are not related to brain maturation.

5.8   Habituation-dishabituation research indicates that
       A.   babies' recall memory is better than their recognition memory.
       B.   infants' memory is facilitated in familiar settings.
       C.   babies do not show evidence of memory for events that take place during infancy.
       D.   participation in the to-be-recalled event hinders memory performance in infancy.

5.9   Recent research suggests that for early memories of events to become autobiographical, the child must
       A.   have a well-developed language system and a repertoire of memory strategies.
       B.   overcome production and utilization deficiencies.
       C.   be attentive to routines and embed novel events in terms of those routines.
       D.   have a well-developed image of the self and the ability to organize personal experiences in narrative form.

5.10   According to Vygotsky, which of the following would be within a child's zone of
       proximal development?
       A.   task that a child cannot accomplish alone or with the help of an adult
       B.   task that a child has recently mastered independently following the
            assistance of an adult
       C.   task that a child cannot yet handle on her own, but can do with the help of
            an adult
       D.   task that a child figures out how to accomplish though her independent
            activity

5.11   Tests of infant intelligence
       A.   show better long-term prediction for high-scoring than for low-scoring
            babies.
       B.   are used largely to help identify infants who are likely to have
            developmental problems in the future.
       C.   are accurate predictors of intelligence during the childhood years.
       D.   help identify those infants who are likely to be intellectually gifted.

5.12   Many researchers believe that the habituation-dishabituation response during
       infancy is effective at predicting later IQ because it
       A.   assesses an important sensorimotor milestone.
       B.   measures a higher-order cognitive skill.
       C.   reveals infants' ability to process complex stimuli.
       D.   taps quickness of thinking, a characteristic of bright individuals.

5.13   Research using the HOME has shown that
       A.   high HOME scores are associated with IQ gains during toddlerhood.
       B.   HOME scores are negatively correlated with mental test performance.
       C.   the strength of the association between HOME and IQ increases from
            infancy to adolescence.
       D.   low HOME scores predict declines as large as 40 to 50 IQ points.

5.14   Which of the following statements concerning child care is NOT true?
       A.   Infants in child care from low-SES homes, but not those from middle-
            SES homes, score lower on tests of cognitive and social skills.
       B.   In all states in the United States, caregivers are required by law to have
            special training in child development.
       C.   Good child care can reduce the negative impact of a stressed, low-SES
            home life.
       D.   In some states in the United States, one adult is permitted to care for up
            to 12 babies at once.

5.15   Which of the following is true regarding graduates of the Carolina Abecedarian
        Project?
        A.   Graduates maintained their IQ advantage over controls well into
              adolescence.
        B.   School-age interventions substantially boosted the children's IQs.
        C.   Nutrition and health services served to foster the children's academic
              achievement.
        D.   Interventions during infancy were not especially effective in boosting
              graduates' mental development.

5.16   According to the nativist perspective, children's rapid acquisition of language is
        due to
        A.   a speech-analyzing neural system that emerges by 1 year of age.
        B.   a series of inborn modules that are specialized for different aspects of
              language acquisition.
        C.   selective reinforcement of children's verbalizations.
        D.   an innate brain mechanism that imposes structure on verbal input.

5.17   Research on babbling shows that
        A.   babies of industrialized cultures begin babbling a few months before
              babies of nonindustrialized cultures.
        B.   sounds of infants' native language are incorporated into their babbling
              even in the absence of exposure to human speech.
        C.   hearing-impaired infants do not babble.
        D.   the early babbling of infants from different language backgrounds is very
              similar.

5.18   One-year-old Fiona uses the word *doggie* to refer only to her family's pet dog and
        not to other dogs. Fiona's error is know as an
        A.   underextension.
        B.   overextension.
        C.   underregularization.
        D.   overregularization.

5.19   Research shows that children with an expressive language style often
        A.   have an especially active interest in exploring objects.
        B.   freely imitate words they hear others say.
        C.   are engaged in social routines by their families.
        D.   have parents who eagerly respond with the names of things to their
              children's first attempts to talk.

5.20   The extent to which ___________ is one of the best predictors of early language
       development and academic achievement during the school years.
       A.   parents engaged their toddlers in conversational give-and-take
       B.   parents' child-directed speech is information-laden
       C.   parents deliberately try to teach infants to talk using child-directed speech
       D.   parents' child-directed speech is made up of exaggerated expression

Chapter 6: Practice Test

6.1　According to Erikson's theory, a mother who promptly and sensitively relieves her infant's discomfort is fostering her baby's sense of
  A.　attachment.
  B.　autonomy.
  C.　trust.
  D.　self.

6.2　An 8-month-old infant is more likely than a 2-month-old infant to
  A.　smile during sleep.
  B.　show no fear when in an unfamiliar situation.
  C.　exhibit generalized distress in response to too much or too little stimulation.
  D.　display anger when a toy is taken away.

6.3　Social referencing is
  A.　the use of a familiar caregiver as a base from which an infant confidently explores the environment and to which the infant returns for emotional support.
  B.　the process of continuously monitoring progress toward a goal, checking outcomes, and redirecting unsuccessful efforts.
  C.　thinking about the self, other people, and social relationships.
  D.　relying on another person's emotional reaction to appraise an uncertain situation.

6.4　Self-conscious emotions appear ___________, as ___________ emerges.
  A.　between 18 and 24 months; self-awareness
  B.　between 12 and 18 months; self-recognition
  C.　between 18 and 24 months; emotional self-regulation
  D.　between 12 and 18 months; the me-self

6.5　Which of the following is NOT an example of emotional self-regulation?
  A.　a child who feels pride because she got good grades on her report card
  B.　an adult who drinks a cup of coffee to wake up in the morning
  C.　an infant who sucks on a pacifier when his feelings get too intense
  D.　a teenager who decides not to watch a scary horror movie

6.6　Which of the following is NOT supported by Thomas and Chess's research?
  A.　Temperament is fixed and unchangeable.
  B.　Temperament is a major factor in the chances that a child will experience psychological problems.
  C.　Temperament can protect children from the effects of a highly stressful home life.
  D.　Parenting practices can modify children's emotional styles.

6.7   Shy, inhibited children
       A.   show greater left frontal brain wave activity than sociable, uninhibited
            children.
       B.   have lower levels of saliva concentration of cortisol than sociable,
            uninhibited children.
       C.   show greater pupil dilation in response to novel stimuli than sociable,
            unhibited children.
       D.   show a drop in blood pressure when faced with novelty.

6.8   Which of the following statements is most accurate?
       A.   Temperament is stable throughout childhood and adolescence.
       B.   Infants who score low or high on characteristics such as shyness and
            sociability are likely to respond similarly when assessed again several
            months to a few years later.
       C.   Temperament is most stable during infancy.
       D.   Temperament is least stable over the long term for those children at the
            extremes--those who are very inhibited or very outgoing.

6.9   Which of the following is NOT supported by research on temperament?
       A.   Children often evoke responses from their caregivers that are consistent
            with parental views and the child's temperamental style.
       B.   When the firstborn child in a family is perceived as having a certain
            temperamental style, all subsequent children are often perceived by the
            parents as having the same temperamental style.
       C.   Mothers' caregiving behaviors often enhance the temperamental styles of
            their infants.
       D.   Gender-stereotyped beliefs often lead parents to promote temperamental
            differences between boys and girls.

6.10   Research with rhesus monkeys reared with terrycloth and wire-mesh "surrogate
       mothers" showed that the infants clung to the
       A.   terrycloth "mother" only when it provided food.
       B.   wire-mesh "mother" only when it provided food.
       C.   terrycloth "mother" regardless of which "mother" provided food.
       D.   wire-mesh "mother" regardless of which "mother" provided food.

6.11   According to Bowlby, infants in the __________ phase, which lasts from
       ____________, develop separation anxiety.
       A.   attachment-in-the-making; 6 weeks to 6 to 8 months
       B.   attachment-in-the-making; 6 to 8 months to 18 to 24 months
       C.   clearcut attachment; 6 weeks to 6 to 8 months
       D.   clearcut attachment; 6 to 8 months to 18 to 24 months

6.12   During the Strange Situation, a parent leaves the room in order to assess
_____________, and returns again to assess the infant's _____________.
   A.   separation anxiety; secure base
   B.   secure base; reaction to the reunion
   C.   separation anxiety; reaction to the reunion
   D.   secure base; separation anxiety

6.13   Rutter's study of institutionalized babies indicates that
   A.   a monotonous sensory environment accounts for the unusual emotional
        and social behavior of these babies.
   B.   children who develop a first attachment bond as late as 4 to 6 years of age
        develop normal emotional and social skills.
   C.   providing institutional infants with enriched visual, auditory, and motor
        stimulation facilitates the development of normal social and emotional
        behaviors.
   D.   fully normal development depends on establishing close bonds with
        caregivers during the first few years of life.

6.14   During the Strange Situation, baby Emmanuel seeks closeness to his mother and
       fails to explore. When his mother returns, Emmanuel cries and displays angry,
       resistive behavior. Emmanuel most likely received _____________ care from her
       mother.
   A.   overstimulating
   B.   unresponsive
   C.   inconsistent
   D.   neglectful

6.15   Research on parents' childhood memories of attachment experiences suggests that
       _____________ is much more influential in how they rear their children than
       _____________.
   A.   the extent to which their own parents engaged in sensitive caregiving;
        their infants' temperament.
   B.   parents' evaluation of their own parents' caregiving style; their own
        beliefs about childcare.
   C.   the way parents view their childhoods; the actual history of care they
        received.
   D.   positive memories of their own childhood experiences; negative
        memories of their own childhood experiences.

6.16   Which of the following is supported by research on mothers' and fathers'
attachment relationships?
   A.   Unemployed mothers engage in more playful stimulation of their babies
        than do employed mothers.
   B.   Fathers who are the primary caregivers tend to be more gender
        stereotyped in their beliefs compared to fathers who are not the primary
        caregivers.
   C.   Mothers', but not fathers', sensitive caregiving predicts attachment
        security.
   D.   Mothers are more likely to engage their infants in conventional games
        such as pat-a-cake and peekaboo, whereas fathers tend to engage in more
        exciting, highly physical games.

6.17   Which of the following is NOT supported by research on siblings' attachment
relationships?
   A.   Coldness in parental relationships is associated with sibling friction.
   B.   Mothers are often less positive and playful with second-borns than first-
        borns--behaviors that can spark feelings of rivalry in the younger child.
   C.   By the second half of the first year, infants are comforted by the presence
        of their brothers or sisters during short absences of the mother.
   D.   Preschoolers often engage in deliberate naughtiness with the arrival of a
        baby brother or sister.

6.18   Research on early child care suggests that each of the following may contribute to
a higher rate of insecure attachment among infants of employed mothers EXCEPT
   A.   more than one child-care arrangement.
   B.   insensitive caregiving at home and in child care.
   C.   full-time employment.
   D.   long hours in child care.

6.19   The ___________ is a sense of self as subject, or agent, who is separate from but
attends to and act on objects and other people.
   A.   I-self
   B.   me-self
   C.   inner-self
   D.   remembered-self

6.20   Around 18 months, the beginnings of self-control first appear in the form of
   A.   benevolence.
   B.   realism.
   C.   compliance.
   D.   reciprocity.

Chapter 7: Practice Test

7.1   During early and middle childhood, X-rays of ___________ permit doctors to
_____________.
    A.   the number of bones and the extent of their ossification; assess children's
motor development
    B.   epiphyses; estimate children's progress toward physical maturity
    C.   the cerebellum; diagnose vitamin and mineral deficiencies
    D.   fontanels; diagnose growth disorders

7.2   Which of the following is NOT supported by research on brain lateralization and
handedness?
    A.   Left-handedness is associated with prenatal and birth difficulties.
    B.   Twins are more likely than ordinary siblings to have the same hand
preference.
    C.   Left-handedness is more frequent among severely retarded and mentally
ill people than.it is in the general population.
    D.   Mixed-handed children are more likely than their right-handed agemates
to develop outstanding verbal and mathematical abilities by adolescence.

7.3   Without treatment, infants born with a deficiency of thyroxine ___________;
whereas at later ages, children with too little thyroxine ___________.
    A.   develop defects in motor functioning and coordination; develop cognitive
difficulties.
    B.   will have very brittle bones that are easily fractured; develop normally
    C.   develop pituitary dwarfism; develop achondroplastic dwarfism
    D.   will be mentally retarded; grow at a below-average rate

7.4   Which of the following is NOT supported by research on nutrition and ordinary
childhood illness, such as measles and chicken pox?
    A.   In undernourished children, ordinary childhood illnesses can hinder
physical growth.
    B.   Illness affects physical growth because it facilitates the body's ability to
absorb foods.
    C.   Ordinary childhood illnesses typically have no effect on physical growth
in well-nourished children.
    D.   Undernourished children are susceptible to disease because poor diet
depresses the body's immune system.

7.5   During the past 30 years, childhood injury deaths have
A.   sharply increased among Western industrialized nations.
B.   declined more rapidly in the United States than in European nations.
C.   increased slightly in the United States, but have declined greatly in most other industrialized countries.
D.   steadily declined in nearly all developed countries, but have dropped only slightly in the United States.

7.6   Which of the following is supported by research on sex differences in motor skills?
A.   Both boys and girls who are exposed to formal training in a range of motor skills develop more rapidly relative to their agemates.
B.   Sex differences in motor skills are largely due to genetically based differences.
C.   Differences in physical capacity between boys and girls increase rapidly beginning in infancy.
D.   Parents tend to foster sex-stereotypic physical activities in their children.

7.7   According to Piaget, which of the following is NOT a change that occurs during the development of make-believe play?
A.   Play becomes increasingly detached from the real-life conditions associated with it.
B.   Pretend actions are first directed at the self and only later toward other objects.
C.   Play includes more and more complex scheme combinations.
D.   Children use increasingly realistic objects as toys during play.

7.8   According to Piaget, the most likely reason that a 4-year-old cannot solve a conservation-of-liquid problem is that
A.   he does not perceive the difference in appearance between the water levels in the two glasses.
B.   the child's attention is captured by the height of the water and she finds it difficult to also consider the widths of the glasses.
C.   the child does not understand that the amount of water in the two glasses is the same prior to the transformation.
D.   the child does not understand the point of the question, Is there the same amount of water in each glass, or does one have more?

7.9   Recent studies indicate that children are LEAST likely to have animistic beliefs about objects that are
A.   distant and unfamiliar, such as clouds or the moon.
B.   familiar in their daily lives, such as crayons and rocks.
C.   able to move by themselves, such as cars and airplanes.
D.   actually alive, such as pets and zoo animals.

7.10 Kim is a Piagetian first-grade teacher who wants all of her students to excel in
      elementary school. What will she do to encourage development?
              A. Allow the children complete freedom to follow their interests.
              B. Have children of different ages collaborate on group projects.
              C. Arrange situations that allow self-paced discovery.
              D. Provide explicit and didactic training in each subject area.

7.11 Unlike Piaget, Vygotsky believed that preschoolers' talking to themselves was
              A. useless.
              B. egocentric.
              C. nonsocial.
              D. self-directing.

7.12 Make-believe play fosters cognitive development in early childhood because it
              A. gives children a rare opportunity to act without self-restraint.
              B. teaches children to rely on private speech to regulate their own behavior.
              C. provides children opportunities to learn to follow internal ideas and social
                  rules rather than their immediate impulses.
              D. teaches children to rely on their own independent efforts rather than on
                  joint activities with adults to solve new tasks.

7.13 One of the major challenges to Vygotsky's theory comes from cross-cultural
      research that shows that, in some cultures,
              A. verbal communication may not be the most important means through
                  which children's thinking develops.
              B. private speech does not precede the development of adultlike dialogues.
              C. make-believe play is not evident in young children's joint, interactive
                  play.
              D. independent discovery learning promotes cognitive development to a
                  greater extent than does joint participation with and verbal guidance by
                  adults.

7.14 Which of the following is NOT supported by research on scripts?
              A. Scripts facilitate children's recall of specific instances of repeated
                  experiences.
              B. Young children's scripts are almost always recalled in the correct
                  sequence.
              C. Children rely on scripts when acting out scenes in make-believe play.
              D. Scripts help children predict what will happen on similar occasions in the
                  future.

7.15 Which of the following is NOT supported by research on theory of mind?
   A. Preschoolers with older siblings are advanced in awareness of false belief.
   B. Children with infantile autism seem to be advanced in mental understanding.
   C. Make-believe play facilitates young children's theory of mind.
   D. Language ability in 4-year-olds predicts mastery of false belief.

7.16 Cross-cultural research on young children's mathematical reasoning suggests that
   A. numbers are represented similarly in all cultures.
   B. informal counting experiences do not facilitate early number understandings.
   C. basic counting knowledge emerges universally around the world.
   D. all children acquire number understandings at the same rate.

7.17 Research shows that young children in __________ score better on assessments of language, academic, motor, and social skills than children in __________.
   A. child-centered preschools; academic preschools
   B. home care; Head Start
   C. academic preschools; child-centered preschools
   D. Head Start; home care

7.18 Research on Head Start has shown that
   A. improvements in IQ and school achievement last throughout the elementary and middle-school years.
   B. one year's intervention is not enough time to boost Head Start children's mental scores.
   C. children remain ahead on measures of real-life school adjustment into adolescence.
   D. children's IQ test scores begin to decline during the first year after entering elementary school.

7.19 According to the principle of mutual exclusivity, when children hear an unfamiliar word, they are most likely to
   A. attach the new word to an object for which they already have a label.
   B. associate the new word with objects that already possess multiple labels.
   C. attach the new word to an unknown object.
   D. associate the new word with familiar words within a familiar category.

7.20 Frances says, "We goed to the circus," and her father replies, "Yes, we went to the circus with your cousin Tony." Her father's reply contains examples of
   A. turnabout and shading.
   B. expansions and turnabout.
   C. recasts and expansions.
   D. shading and recasts.

Chapter 8: Practice Test

8.1   According to Erikson, the negative outcome of early childhood is an overly
      A. strict superego.
      B. indulgent id.
      C. indifferent ego.
      D. restrained id.

8.2   Two distinct aspects of the self that emerge during the preschool years and become more refined with age are
      A. the I-self and the me-self.
      B. inter-cognition and intra-cognition.
      C. material qualities and physical qualities.
      D. semantic thoughts and episodic thoughts.

8.3   Preschoolers tend to rate their own self-esteem as extremely __________ and __________ the difficult of tasks.
      A. low; overestimate
      B. low, underestimate
      C. high; overestimate
      D. high; underestimate

8.4   In their preschool classroom, Lucy accidentally tripped and spilled her plate of spaghetti. Thinking this was funny, Sam grabbed a handful of his spaghetti and threw it on the floor. Which of the following statements is true?
      A. Lucy, but not Sam, is likely to feel guilty.
      B. Sam, but not Lucy, is likely to feel guilty.
      C. Both Lucy and Sam are likely to feel guilty.
      D. Neither Lucy nor Sam is likely to feel guilty.

8.5   Which of the following is supported by research on play in early childhood?
      A. Nonsocial activity is the most frequent form of play among 3- to 4-year-olds.
      B. From 3 to 6 years, the frequency of parallel play increases with age.
      C. By kindergarten age, children rarely engage in nonsocial activity.
      D. From 3 to 6 years, the frequency of solitary play decreases with age.

8.6   Four-year-old Oliver and his friends often pretend to search for monsters in a magical forest. These episodes of sociodramatic play are likely to
      A. hinder Oliver's emotional self-regulatory skills.
      B. strengthen Oliver's wariness of the woods.
      C. help Oliver to be less afraid of the woods.
      D. strengthen Oliver's fear of unfamiliar situations.

8.7   Preschoolers tend to view friendships in terms of
        A.   personal qualities.
        B.   shared activities.
        C.   mutual trust.
        D.   physical proximity.

8.8   Parents who phrase their directives positively and politely tend to have
        preschoolers who
        A.   have trouble regulating negative emotion.
        B.   are successful in influencing peers.
        C.   have trouble initiating play with peers.
        D.   are highly susceptible to peer pressure.

8.9   According to Freud's theory, morality emerges in children
        A.   during the genital stage.
        B.   at the beginning of the Oedipus and Electra conflicts.
        C.   through the threat of punishment from the opposite-sex parent.
        D.   by identifying with the same-sex parent and internalizing his or her moral
             standards.

8.10   Which of the following is NOT supported by research on modeling?
        A.   When models say one thing and do another, children tend to imitate the
             most lenient standard of behavior adults demonstrate.
        B.   Children are more willing to copy the behavior of agemates than that of
             older peers and adults.
        C.   Once children acquire a moral response, the frequency of reinforcement
             increases.
        D.   Models are more influential on children's prosocial behavior during the
             preschool years than during the school years.

8.11   The cognitive-developmental view of moral development emphasizes
        A.   the role of brain lateralization and syntactic pruning in promoting
             cognitive skills needed for moral thought.
        B.   the child's internalization of moral societal standards.
        C.   forms of discipline that encourage and reward good conduct.
        D.   children as active thinker about social rules.

8.12   Lenny says, "Elton is a loser, so don't talk to him." This is an example of
        ___________ aggression.
        A.   instrumental
        B.   overt
        C.   relational
        D.   antagonistic

8.13   Which of the following is supported by research on aggression?
    A.   Preschool and school-age girls are less aggressive than boys.
    B.   Girls resort to relational aggression more often than boys do.
    C.   Hostile aggression decreases with age as children become better at detecting others' intensions.
    D.   Boys are more overtly aggressive than girls in the United States, but not in non-Western cultures.

8.14   Research on television violence indicates that violent TV
    A.   strengthens hostility in highly aggressive children.
    B.   makes children less willing to tolerate aggression in others.
    C.   does not cause difficulties in parent and peer relations.
    D.   is rare in cartoons and other children's shows.

8.15   Which of the following is NOT supported by research on gender typing?
    A.   Mothers tend to label emotions when talking to their sons and explain emotions when talking to their daughters.
    B.   Parents' differential expectations and perceptions of their sons and daughters begin at birth.
    C.   Parents are more likely to describe achievement as important for their sons and close supervision of activities as important for their daughters.
    D.   Parents tend to react more positively when their son demands attention than when their daughter does.

8.16   Which of the following is supported by research on gender typing and play during the preschool years?
    A.   Boys are more intolerant than girls of cross-gender play.
    B.   Preschoolers often engage in "gender-inappropriate" activities during play.
    C.   Preschoolers play in mixed-gender groups more than they play in same-sex groups.
    D.   Boys who frequently engage in "gender-inappropriate" activities are likely to be ignored by other boys even when they engage in "masculine" activities.

8.17   Which of the following children is most likely to have the lowest self-esteem?
    A.   Madeline, who has a "feminine" identity
    B.   Oscar, who has an "androgynous" identity
    C.   Max, who has a "masculine" identity
    D.   Elizabeth, who has an "androgynous" identity

8.18 Four-year-old Athena's mother often tells her that "cars and trucks are for boys."
According to gender schema theory, Athena is likely to
    A. avoid playing with cars and trucks.
    B. ask her father to play cars and trucks with her.
    C. be resentful when she sees other girls playing with cars and trucks.
    D. seek out opportunities to play with boys who are playing with cars and trucks.

8.19 Physical discipline in early childhood predicts aggression during the school years
    A. for all children.
    B. only for African-American children.
    C. only for Hispanic children.
    D. only for Caucasian-American children.

8.20 Parents Anonymous combats child maltreatment by providing
    A. access to health care.
    B. social supports.
    C. clean and noncrowded living conditions.
    D. low-cost, high-quality child care.

Chapter 9: Practice Test

9.1   During middle childhood, the ___________ is growing fastest.
   A.   head
   B.   top portion of the body
   C.   trunk
   D.   lower portion of the body

9.2   Next to prior obesity, which of the following is the best predictor of future obesity among school-age children?
   A.   time spent in front of the television
   B.   obese parents
   C.   low familial income
   D.   parents who use food to reward good behavior

9.3   Which of the following is NOT supported by research on unintentional injuries in middle childhood?
   A.   Bicycle accidents are the leading cause of injury in middle childhood.
   B.   The rate of injury deaths increases from middle childhood into adolescence.
   C.   In middle childhood, those at the greatest risk for injury have parents who use punitive or inconsistent discipline.
   D.   Bicycle injuries in middle childhood most often occur from disobeying traffic rules.

9.4   Which of the following is supported by research on sex differences in motor skills during middle childhood?
   A.   Boys are more advanced than girls in fine motor skills.
   B.   Girls outperform boys on skills that depend on agility and balance.
   C.   Boys' genetic advantage in muscle mass accounts for their superiority in most gross motor skills.
   D.   Boys are ahead of girls on all gross motor skills.

9.5   Research on physical education suggests that schools should
   A.   have more lenient fitness standards.
   B.   place more emphasis on competitive sports.
   C.   have fewer physical education requirements.
   D.   offer more frequent opportunities for informal games.

9.6   Piaget regarded conservation as the single most important achievement of the concrete operational stage because it provides clear evidence of
   A.   propositional thinking.
   B.   operations.
   C.   abstract thinking.
   D.   hypothetico-deductive reasoning.

9.7   Research that shows that conservation is often delayed in tribal and village societies challenges Piaget's assumption that operational thinking
A.   is largely the result of school practices.
B.   is not achieved by nonindustrialized cultures.
C.   is directly responsible for language acquisition.
D.   emerges spontaneously as the result children's self-exploration of the world.

9.8   According to information-processing theorists, cognitive inhibition supports many information-processing skills by
A.   increasing the size of the long-term memory.
B.   clearing unnecessary information from working memory.
C.   enhancing the capacity of the sensory register.
D.   aiding with retrieval from long-term memory.

9.9   To help her remember the words *soup*, *hat*, and *bird*, Fatma generated a mental image of a bird drinking soup out of a hat. In this example, Fatma is using a memory strategy referred to as
A.   rehearsal.
B.   association.
C.   elaboration.
D.   organization.

9.10   Cross-cultural research indicates that people in non-Western cultures who have no formal schooling
A.   do not use or benefit from instruction in memory strategies.
B.   do less well than formally schooled people on tasks that require memory for spatial location and arrangement of objects.
C.   have a more difficult time than formally schooled people using memory cues that are available in everyday life.
D.   memorize information much in the same way that schooled, Western individuals do.

9.11   __________ is the process of monitoring progress toward a goal, checking outcomes, and redirecting unsuccessful efforts.
A.   Metacognitive knowledge
B.   Cognitive inhibition
C.   Cognitive self-regulation
D.   Theory of mind

9.12 Teachers who advocate a whole-language approach argue that
      A. from the beginning, children should be exposed to text in its complete form.
      B. reading instruction should focus on coaching in phonics.
      C. first, children should learn the basic rules for translating written symbols into sounds.
      D. young children should be given simplified text materials.

9.13 Cross-cultural research suggests that American math instruction may have gone too far in emphasizing
      A. back-up strategies.
      B. computer-assisted instruction (CAI).
      C. computational drill.
      D. numerical understanding.

9.14 __________ is a statistical procedure used for studying the underlying mental abilities associated with intelligence tests.
      A. Regression analysis
      B. Analysis of variance
      C. Correlational analysis
      D. Factor analysis

9.15 On IQ tests in which fact-oriented verbal items are eliminated and only spatial reasoning and performance tasks are used,
      A. low-SES minority children perform as well as their white middle-SES agemates.
      B. the scores of low-SES minority children drop relative to their scores on tests that emphasize only fact-oriented, verbal tasks.
      C. low-SES minority children still perform more poorly than their white middle-SES agemates.
      D. low-SES minority children perform substantially better compared to their white middle-SES agemates.

9.16 Recent research shows that bilingual children
      A. in the United States often receive support for their native language in school.
      B. exhibit cognitive and linguistic deficits.
      C. do better than their single-language agemates on tests of analytic reasoning and concept formation.
      D. generally take about a year to become as fluent in a second language as native-speaking agemates.

9.17 Which of the following is supported by research on traditional versus open
classrooms?
  A. Compared to children in traditional classrooms, those in open classrooms
     are viewed as relatively passive in the learning process.
  B. Kindergartners display more stress behaviors in open than in traditional
     classrooms.
  C. Children in open classrooms have a slight edge in academic achievement
     over those in traditional classrooms.
  D. Compared to children in traditional classrooms, those in open classrooms
     show greater gains in critical thinking.

9.18 Which of the following is NOT supported by research on teacher-pupil
interactions?
  A. When teachers hold inaccurate views, high achievers are more affected
     than low achievers.
  B. High-achieving pupils experience more positive interaction with their
     teachers than do low-achieving pupils.
  C. Children who achieve poorly and are disruptive are rarely called on
     during class discussions.
  D. Teacher opinion can influence children's performance in school.

9.19 The Individuals with Disabilities Education Act mandates that schools
  A. extend mainstreaming of students with learning disabilities to full
     inclusion.
  B. place children with learning disabilities in the least restrictive
     environments that meet their educational needs.
  C. mainstream only those pupils who have difficulties with more than one
     aspect of learning.
  D. provide students access to educators who are specialized in teaching
     children with learning disabilities.

9.20 Cross-cultural research shows that as they move up through the grades in school,
American children __________ relative to children in other countries such as
Hong Kong, Japan, Korea, and Taiwan.
  A. drop in mathematics and science achievement
  B. increase in mathematics and science achievement
  C. decrease in reading achievement
  D. increase in reading achievement

Chapter 10: Practice Test

10.1   According to Erikson, during middle childhood, children are at risk for developing a sense of _________ when their teachers and peers are so negative that they destroy their feelings of competency and mastery.
      A.   guilt
      B.   shame
      C.   mistrust
      D.   inferiority

10.2   Studies of self-esteem indicate that it
      A.   rises dramatically as soon as children enter elementary school.
      B.   increases steadily throughout the school years and then falls during the last couple of years of high school.
      C.   is very high during early childhood and then drops over the first few years of elementary school.
      D.   remains stable during early childhood and elementary school and then plunges during middle school.

10.3   Mastery-oriented attributions credit success to _________ and failure to _________.
      A.   high ability; insufficient ability
      B.   high effort; insufficient ability
      C.   high ability; insufficient effort
      D.   high effort; insufficient effort

10.4   Each of the following is supported by research on emotional understanding EXCEPT
      A.   in middle childhood, children can reconcile contradictory facial and situational cues in figuring out another's feelings.
      B.   in middle childhood, children can use a person's past experiences to predict how he or she will feel in a new situation.
      C.   in middle childhood, children report guilt for both intentional and unintentional wrongdoings.
      D.   in middle childhood, children recognize that they can experience more than one emotion at a time.

10.5   Damon's sequence of distributive justice reasoning is as follows:
      A.   merit, equality, and benevolence.
      B.   equality, merit, and benevolence.
      C.   benevolence, equality, and merit.
      D.   merit, benevolence, and equality.

10.6   When children and adolescents challenge parental authority, they typically do so
        within the ___________ domain.
   A.   moral
   B.   social-conventional
   C.   personal
   D.   relational

10.7   Which of the following is NOT typically a characteristic of peer groups?
   A.   unique values and standards of behavior
   B.   decreased relational aggression and antisocial behavior toward peer
        group members
   C.   a social structure of leaders and followers
   D.   loyalty to collective goals

10.8   Which of the following is NOT supported by research on children's friendships?
   A.   Trust becomes a defining feature of friendships during middle
        childhood.
   B.   Girls are more exclusive in their friendships than are boys.
   C.   School-age children are more selective about their friendships than are
        preschoolers.
   D.   School-age children report having more friends than do preschoolers.

10.9   Rejected-aggressive children
   A.   are passive and socially awkward.
   B.   tend to be deficient in social understanding.
   C.   are very concerned about being scorned and attacked.
   D.   hold negative expectation for how peers will treat them.

10.10   Raymond has been classifed as controversial. Which of the following
        characteristics is he LEAST likely to have?
   A.   happy and comfortable with peer relationships
   B.   disliked by a large number of peers
   C.   hostile and disruptive
   D.   socially awkward

10.11   Both adults and children are likely to view which of the following activities as
        just as bad as violating a moral rule?
   A.   Five-year-old Charlene pretending to shave like her father.
   B.   Five-year-old Maria wearing her mother's high-heel shoes.
   C.   Five-year-old Marcella playing with toy soldiers.
   D.   Five-year-old Thomas playing house.

10.12   Cross-cultural research in Kenya suggests that Nyansongo girls score higher than girls of other village and tribal cultures in dominance, assertiveness, and playful roughhousing because
    A.   the entire Nyansongo family engages in "masculine" activities such as hunting and fishing.
    B.   traits such as freedom and independence are directly taught to and reinforced in Nyansongo girls.
    C.   children of both sexes perform "feminine" activities such as tending to the cooking fire and care of young children.
    D.   Nyansongo boys take on the entire responsibility of caregiving and preparing meals.

10.13   Each of the following is a critical ingredient of coregulation EXCEPT
    A.   children must be willing to imform parents of their whereabouts, activities, and problems.
    B.   parents must monitor, guide, and support their children at a distance.
    C.   children must be willing to defer to parents for decisions that involve risk-taking behavior.
    D.   parents must strengthen in their children abilities that will allow them to monitor their own behavior.

10.14   Sibling rivalry tends to be especially strong
    A.   among siblings who are close in age.
    B.   when siblings strive to be different from one another.
    C.   among different-sex siblings.
    D.   when mothers prefer one child.

10.15   Compared with agemates who have siblings, only children
    A.   exhibit higher rates of hyperactive, inattentive, and impulsive behavior.
    B.   tend to be less popular with peers.
    C.   have poorer social skills.
    D.   do better in school and attain higher levels of education.

10.16   According to research on divorce, who is MOST likely to experience serious adjustment problems?
    A.   Max, whose mother has custody
    B.   Steve, whose father has custody
    C.   Rachel, whose mother has custody
    D.   Melissa, whose father has custody

10.17   The overriding factor in positive adjustment following divorce is
        A.   effective parenting.
        B.   children's cognitive and social maturity.
        C.   children's relationships with extended family, teachers, and friends.
        D.   children's temperament.

10.18   Research shows that maternal employment
        A.   reduces the time school-age children spend with their mothers.
        B.   hinders academic achievement.
        C.   tends to create increased gender-stereotyped beliefs in children.
        D.   results in more time with fathers for school-age children.

10.19   The typical child who displays a school phobia is
        A.   a student with low academic achievement or a learning disability.
        B.   a pupil with exceedingly low self-esteem and poor social skills.
        C.   a kindergartner or first grader who is afraid to leave his or her mother.
        D.   middle-class, with above-average grades.

10.20   Research on child sexual abuse indicates that
        A.   both boys and girls are equally likely to be sexually abused.
        B.   reported cases are highest in early childhood and adolescence.
        C.   the abuser is most often a parent or someone the parent knows well.
        D.   most sexually abused children experience only a single incident.

Chapter 11: Practice Test

11.1   According to Freud, adolescence
        A.   involves a reawakening of the struggle of the phallic stage.
        B.   is a period of calm after the storm of middle childhood.
        C.   corresponds to the phallic stage of psychosexual development.
        D.   is a period of harmony and predictability of behaviors.

11.2   Which of the following statements is true of physical skill in adolescence?
        A.   Boys and girls are evenly matched.
        B.   Only the highest performing girls have skills equal to the average boy.
        C.   Low performing girls have skills equal to high performing boys.
        D.   Girls perform better in athletics until about age 15, when boys surpass them.

11.3   All of the adolescent girls below are the same age. Who will probably be the first to reach menarche?
        A.   Tania, a long distance runner
        B.   Brooke, who is overweight
        C.   Imarin, who comes from a low-income family and is malnourished
        D.   Marina, who suffers from frequent illness

11.4   The primary factor that causes adolescents to experience more mood shifts than adults seems to be
        A.   more frequent changes in their environmental situation.
        B.   more drastic shifts in the levels of hormones in their blood.
        C.   the instability of the emotional control structures in the brain.
        D.   a cognitive inability to understand or control their feelings.

11.5   Which school setting would have the greatest chance of preventing delinquency in early maturing girls?
        A.   a combination middle-high school
        B.   an all-girl, K-6 school
        C.   a K-6 school
        D.   a program that allows early maturing children to take classes with older peers to enhance their self-esteem

11.6   The most common nutritional problem of adolescence is a deficiency in
        A.   calcium.
        B.   protein.
        C.   iron.
        D.   zinc.

11.7   Lorna, an anorexic teenager, has lost so much weight that her bones show clearly, her hair is falling out, and she has stopped menstruating. When she looks in the mirror, Lorna is likely to think,
  A.   "I really like the way I look now."
  B.   "I just need to lose 10 more pounds."
  C.   "If only I could put weight back on."
  D.   "Now my parents will be proud of me."

11.8   Which of the following characteristics has NOT been linked to early teenage sexual activity?
  A.   parental divorce
  B.   poor school performance
  C.   small family size
  D.   tendency to engage in norm-violating acts

11.9   Research into the causes of homosexuality has found evidence for the influence of
  A.   overly strict parenting during the early years.
  B.   a gene or group of genes on the X chromosome.
  C.   excessive contact with homosexual adults.
  D.   chemical pollutants found in the atmosphere.

11.10   All of the statements below are true of teenage mothers EXCEPT
  A.   they have fewer complications during pregnancy due to age.
  B.   they often have additional out-of-wedlock births in quick succession.
  C.   they are more likely to divorce if they do marry.
  D.   they have a 50 percent likelihood of dropping out of school.

11.11   Teenagers who are at the highest risk for sexually transmitted diseases are
  A.   mid-SES teens whose parents are very permissive.
  B.   low-SES teens who feel a sense of hopelessness.
  C.   high-achieving teens whose parents are demanding.
  D.   high-SES teens who are future oriented.

11.12   Which of these is the most consistent predictor of adolescent substance abuse?
  A.   low income levels
  B.   parental drug use
  C.   poor grades in school
  D.   peer influences

11.13   Bonnie is concrete operational and Katie is formal operational. When asked to
solve the pendulum problem, Bonnie will
      A.   be completely unable to solve the problem.
      B.   systematically test alternative hypotheses.
      C.   solve it intuitively, without experimentation.
      D.   unsystematically test the variables affecting the pendulum speed.

11.14   Young children are unable to grasp the _____ of propositional reasoning—that
the validity of conclusions drawn from premises rests on the rules of logic, not
on real-world confirmation.
      A.   obvious contradictions
      B.   concrete examples
      C.   logical necessity
      D.   single foundation

11.15   According to the information-processing view, which of the following is NOT
an accurate statement of how scientific reasoning develops.
      A.   It develops in a step-by-step fashion.
      B.   Adolescents master component skills in sequential order and combine
them into a smoothly functioning system.
      C.   Scientific reasoning develops gradually out of many specific
experiences.
      D.   Scientific reasoning is directly taught in the higher grades

11.16   Although Suzanna desperately wants to learn how to dive, she refuses to practice
at the pool because "everyone will be watching me and laugh because I'm the
only one who can't do it." Her thinking reflects
      A.   the imaginary audience.
      B.   the personal fable.
      C.   idealism.
      D.   cognitive self-regulation.

11.17   An important factor that contributes to the gender difference in mathematical
performance is that
      A.   boys think math is less useful to their future lives.
      B.   girls think of math as a masculine domain.
      C.   girls believe you don't have to work hard at math.
      D.   girls better understand the practical importance of math.

11.18   Students are at especially great risk for academic and emotional difficulties after
a school transition if they
      A.   move from a larger school to a smaller one.
      B.   had higher grades before the move.
      C.   have to cope with added life transitions.
      D.   come from a school with eight grades under one roof.

11.19   Research has shown that inner-city African-American adolescents who are high-achieving and optimistic about their futures in the face of peer pressures
   A.   have an unrealistic world view.
   B.   developed the philosophy that injustice can be overcome through discussions with parents, relatives, and teachers.
   C.   are targets of school violence.
   D.   tend to complete high school, but drop out of college.

11.20   A high school student who is involved in extracurricular activities will generally
   A.   show poorer performance on academic subjects.
   B.   be less likely to drop out of high school.
   C.   be more likely to drop out of high school.
   D.   feel more negative effects of peer pressure.

Chapter 12: Practice Test

12.1   According to current theorists, a typical adolescent's approach to forming a
mature identity is characterized by
        A.   exploration.
        B.   crisis.
        C.   commitment.
        D.   basic trust.

12.2   Leslie is unable to select a vocation that matches her interests and skills. She
probably
        A.   has a weak sense of trust.
        B.   has little autonomy.
        C.   lacks a sense of industry.
        D.   has no initiative.

12.3   Which statement below exemplifies an adolescent's awareness that psychological
qualities often change from one situation to the next?
        A.   "I have a fairly good sense of humor."
        B.   "I'm smart."
        C.   "I'm not shy."
        D.   "I think I'm a good person."

12.4   When asked about his career plans, Simon says, "Haven't thought about it.
Doesn't make too much difference what I do." He is characterized by
        A.   identity achievement.
        B.   identity diffusion.
        C.   moratorium.
        D.   identity foreclosure.

12.5   Which of the following is NOT something that schools can do to facilitate the
development of mature identities among students?
        A.   promote higher-level thinking skills
        B.   encourage low-SES students to go to college
        C.   increase the numbers of remedial classes to support slow learners
        D.   provide vocational training that immerses students in real work
            situations

12.6   In Piaget's autonomous morality stage, children typically
        A.   realize people can have different perspectives on moral matters.
        B.   view moral rules as unchangeable, requiring strict obedience.
        C.   base their judgments on physical actions, not on intentions.
        D.   believe that others hold the same moral views as themselves.

12.7   In response to the Heinz dilemma, Maria says, "The law was written to protect
         people, but in this case it's hurting his wife. So he should steal it, since by
         breaking the law he is really following its original meaning." She is at which of
         Kohlberg's stages of moral development?
         A.   Stage 3
         B.   Stage 4
         C.   Stage 5
         D.   Stage 6

12.8   One of Kohlberg's stages represents a reflective, philosophical orientation that
         lies beyond the realm of commonplace, spontaneous moral thought. As a result,
         there is no clear evidence of its existence. Which stage is this?
         A.   Stage 1
         B.   Stage 3
         C.   Stage 4
         D.   Stage 6

12.9   Questioning the universality of Kohlberg's stages, researchers studying East
         Indian participants found all of the following EXCEPT that
         A.   only people in the United States reach the highest moral levels.
         B.   just as many as or more Indians as Americans reached the
              postconventional level.
         C.   East Indian participants often dealt with moral conflicts in ways that
              did not fit into Kohlberg's scheme.
         D.   Kohlberg's theory does not capture all aspects of moral thinking in
              every culture.

12.10   Recent research that measures the moral development of males and females with
         both hypothetical and real-life moral dilemmas finds that
         A.   females fall behind males only on real-life dilemmas.
         B.   both sexes emphasize justice and caring reasoning.
         C.   females fall behind males in development.
         D.   males fall behind females in development.

12.11   Which child is likely to be psychologically healthier?
         A.   Maria, who has a strong feminine gender identity
         B.   Luis, who has a strong masculine gender identity
         C.   Gabriella, who has an androgynous gender identity
         D.   Gordon, who has a strong feminine gender identity

12.12   Parent-child relations in adolescence can be better understood if we keep in mind that
        A.   parents have very different gender stereotypes than adolescents.
        B.   both parents and teenagers are undergoing major life transitions.
        C.   teenagers are focused on their families more than ever before.
        D.   adolescents have not yet achieved formal operational thinking.

12.13   When asked about the meaning of friendship, teenagers stress which of the following characteristics?
        A.   attractiveness and popularity
        B.   common interests and activities
        C.   intimacy and loyalty
        D.   kindness and happiness

12.14   Research findings regarding cultural variations in group norms indicate that
        A.   many peer group values are extensions of those acquired at home.
        B.   peer pressure is much more intense in the United States than in other countries.
        C.   adolescents worldwide value the same characteristics.
        D.   differences noted among peer groups in different areas of the United States are more pronounced than among adolescents in different areas of the world.

12.15   The first dating relationships of homosexual youths tend to be short-lived and involve little emotional commitment because
        A.   they are not emotionally ready for more involved relationships.
        B.   they are still questioning their sexual identity.
        C.   they fear peer harassment and rejection.
        D.   they are looking for relationships that are purely fun and nothing else.

12.16   Adolescents are most likely to conform to peer expectations in matters such as
        A.   the type of clothing they wear.
        B.   whether or not they go to college.
        C.   their basic moral values.
        D.   the overall plans they make for their lives.

12.17   ______ are much more prone to depression.
        A.   Early maturing girls
        B.   Girls with androgynous gender-role identities
        C.   Girls with masculine gender-role identities
        D.   Early maturing boys

12.18 Which of the following cognitive characteristics of adolescents contributes most
directly to the sharp rise in suicide from childhood to adolescence?
   A. personal fable
   B. impulsiveness
   C. emotional distance from parents
   D. school environments

12.19 The larger numbers of boys who commit violent offenses can be directly traced
to
   A. angry, inconsistent discipline during childhood.
   B. gender discrimination among teachers.
   C. ostracization by peers during preschool.
   D. cranky and irritable behavior as a baby.

12.20 A treatment program for serious delinquents will typically be more effective if it
   A. focuses all its efforts on the cause of the delinquency.
   B. teaches social skills needed to deal with difficulties.
   C. emphasizes the individual rather than a group.
   D. is intense but brief, rather than drawn out.

Chapter 13: Practice Test

13.1   Which of the following does NOT occur after body structures reach maximum capacity and efficiency in the teens and twenties?
        A.   biological aging
        B.   senescence
        C.   gender intensification
        D.   genetically influenced declines in the functioning of organs and systems

13.2   Which of the following was NOT a finding of the "Termite" study?
        A.   The combined effects of personality and parental divorce on length of life are greater than the effect of gender.
        B.   Cheerful, happy-go-lucky children grew into adults who engaged in risky behaviors.
        C.   Lasting effects of divorce were not overcome by remarriage.
        D.   Cheerful, happy-go-lucky children lived longer than their conscientious peers.

13.3   For most people, the maximum lifespan falls within the range of
        A.   50 to 80 years.
        B.   70 to 110 years.
        C.   110 to 130 years.
        D.   85 to 90 years.

13.4   The average active lifespan for Americans is
        A.   just under 50 years.
        B.   64 years.
        C.   70 years.
        D.   between 85 to 90 years.

13.5   The strongest evidence to support the "genetic programming" theory is
        A.   the increase in DNA breaks and cellular deletions and damage with age.
        B.   the release of free radicals by the body.
        C.   telomeres are lost after each cell division, resulting in a maximum cell lifespan of approximately 50 divisions.
        D.   that the cross-linkage of protein fibers in connective tissue can be reduced by exercise and diet.

13.6   When an adult suffers from atherosclerosis, or deposits of fatty plaque on the walls of the arteries, it typically develops
        A.   very slightly before age 60, but can become serious after that.
        B.   after age 40 in individuals who showed no signs of it earlier.
        C.   very rapidly in extreme old age, leading to sudden heart failure.
        D.   in early adulthood and progresses to become a serious illness.

13.7   Longitudinal research with several hundred thousand participants revealed that young and middle-aged adults at low risk for heart disease had death rates reduced by
    A.   40 to 60 percent.
    B.   10 to 20 percent.
    C.   30 to 50 percent.
    D.   70 to 80 percent.

13.8   Juan is a tennis player; Miguel is a golfer. Which statement below is correct?
    A.   Both athletes' skills will peak in their early twenties.
    B.   Juan's athletic skills will peak in his early thirties.
    C.   Miguel's skills will peak in his late twenties or early thirties.
    D.   Both athletes' skills will peak in their late thirties.

13.9   Compared with people of normal weight, obese individuals are more likely to be
    A.   victims of severe hormonal imbalances.
    B.   cheerful and optimistic in outlook on life.
    C.   middle- or upper- income individuals.
    D.   denied apartments, college loans, and jobs.

13.10   Regular physical activity benefits people by
    A.   reducing skin cancer rates.
    B.   reducing all kinds of cholesterol.
    C.   increasing resistance to illness.
    D.   increasing stress responses.

13.11   Among men, alcholism generally begins ______, while among women it generally begins ______.
    A.   with hard liquor; with wine
    B.   with wine; with hard liquor
    C.   in the teens and early twenties; in the twenties and thirties
    D.   in the twenties and thirties; in the teens and early twenties

13.12   In general, as the number of sexual partners a person has goes up, the person's sexual satisfaction
    A.   increases sharply.
    B.   increases slightly.
    C.   stays the same.
    D.   decreases sharply.

13.13   In a national study of over 6000 college students, _____ of the women reported
having experienced sexual coercion, and _____ of the men reported having
obtained sex through force.
    A.   50 percent; 50 percent
    B.   44 percent; 19 percent
    C.   20 percent; 50 percent
    D.   20 percent; nearly two-thirds

13.14   Moniqua has just moved to another city after her divorce and is dealing with
stress. Which of the following suggestions would have the highest probability of
helping her to buffer the effects of stress?
    A.   hit the singles clubs and bars after work
    B.   actively seek out a satisfying sexual relationship
    C.   take antidepressants
    D.   develop and maintain satisfying social ties

13.15   In Perry's study of adult thinking, older students engaged in relativistic thought,
in which they
    A.   insisted that their own ideas were necessarily the right ones.
    B.   saw all information as either good or bad, right or wrong.
    C.   accepted multiple truths, each relative to its own context.
    D.   accepted all information that came from authority figures.

13.16   Barbara is a musician, Chris is an artist, and Dennis is an engineer. Which of the
following statements is probably true?
    A.   Dennis's creativity will peak later than that of the other two.
    B.   Chris's creativity will be the last to peak.
    C.   Barbara will be the last to show a rise in creativity.
    D.   Creativity will diminish equally among all three people.

13.17   In the Seattle Longitudinal Study, findings on five mental abilities showed
    A.   no trends in mental abilities at any age.
    B.   a slow, steady increase in abilities.
    C.   a cross-sectional drop in abilities after age 35.
    D.   large fluctuations in abilities at all ages.

13.18   College attendance will have the most psychological impact on which student?
    A.   Terryn, who attends a four-year institution and lives at home
    B.   Sara, who attends a four-year institution and lives on campus
    C.   Kristen, who attends a two-year institution and lives at home
    D.   Allyson, who attends a prestigious university and commutes

13.19   Twenty-year-old Dominic explored the possibility of becoming a teacher by
        tutoring in an after-school program. He then chose to major in education.
        Dominic is in the ______ of vocational development.
        A. fantasy period
        B. tentative period
        C. realistic period
        D. acquisition period

13.20   The author argues that the involvement of government and society in preparing
        young people for careers should be
        A. limited to the most needy, unemployable youths.
        B. severely restricted to protect individual rights.
        C. secondary to their own and their family's efforts.
        D. expanded to help them become productive citizens.

Chapter 14: Practice Test

14.1   Anna defines her identity in terms of being a wife. She has less self-respect now than she did in her early twenties and has little initiative. Which of the following is probably true?
A.   Anna has not balanced intimacy and isolation in her life, and depends too heavily on intimacy.
B.   Anna has not balanced intimacy and isolation in her life and leans too heavily towards isolation.
C.   Anna's husband has perfectly balanced the intimacy and isolation forces in his life.
D.   Anna has successfully maneuvered through the intimacy versus isolation conflict.

14.2   Levinson said that the structure-building periods of adult development are primarily focused on
A.   determining the long-term goals a person wants from life.
B.   creating relationships with the important people in one's life.
C.   figuring out the kind of identity a person will be creating.
D.   selecting and integrating components to achieve one's goals.

14.3   According to Levinson's theory of adult development, which individual is most likely to be in a stage of settling down and advancing?
A.   Leslie, a 30-year old nurse
B.   Tony, a 35-year-old engineer
C.   Ida, a 33-year old teacher
D.   Ken, a 25-year-old doctoral student

14.4   According to Vaillant's theory of adult development, men in their fifties tended to become
A.   depressed and unsatisfied with their lives.
B.   more and more focused on their careers.
C.   more interested in their wives and family.
D.   "keepers of meaning" for their culture.

14.5   All the women in Sophia's book club followed some sort of social clock. They are all probably
A.   timid and conforming.
B.   limited in their life options.
C.   more confident and secure.
D.   not representative of the larger sample of women.

14.6   Which component of love involves the recognition that one is in love and the decision to maintain that relationship?
A. commitment
B. intimacy
C. passion
D. control

14.7   One of the strongest predictors of marital distress and future divorce is
A. maintaining each person's separate identity.
B. the escalation of negative interaction sparked by criticism, contempt, defensiveness, and stonewalling.
C. lack of creativity in sexual activities.
D. maintaining one's individual friends and activities.

14.8   Which is true of the differences in friendships between men and women?
A. Men have more intimate same-sex friendships than women do.
B. Women are reluctant to divulge information about themselves in the fear that their friends may not reciprocate.
C. Women prefer to "do something" when they get together.
D. Men feel competition with male friends and are unwilling to disclose any weaknesses.

14.9   Compared with in adolescence, interactions with siblings in early adulthood tend to be
A. an increasing source of tension.
B. less important and more distant.
C. more frequent and friendlier.
D. related to developing romances.

14.10   If they are all statistically average, which of these people is most likely to be lonely?
A. Janine, who is 30 years old and has never married
B. Miguel, who is 50 years old and has recently married
C. Barbara, who is 25 years old and was just divorced
D. Steven, who is 40 years old and has been married for 20 years

14.11   Young people who have moved out of the house are least likely to return home to live if they moved out because of
A. getting married.
B. family disagreements.
C. going to college.
D. joining the military.

14.12   When the first child is born into a family, what effect does this typically have on
the parents' gender roles?
    A.   It makes their gender roles more traditional.
    B.   It makes their gender roles less traditional.
    C.   It makes them both become more feminine.
    D.   It makes them both become less feminine.

14.13   Research on over 2,000 couples has shown that the strongest predictor of
parenting satisfaction is
    A.   SES.
    B.   age of the mother when the first child was born.
    C.   educational level of the father.
    D.   marital quality.

14.14   One important difference between cohabiting couples and couples who are
married or living in separate residences is that cohabitors are more likely to
    A.   feel a strong commitment to their partners.
    B.   be more liberal and unconventional.
    C.   be politically conservative and religious.
    D.   have warm, close ties with their parents.

14.15   Which couple will likely be the most content with their lives?
    A.   Kaipo and Noelani, who are voluntarily childless
    B.   Kevin and Nicole, who do not have children due to infertility
    C.   Kyle and Nyree, whose son is autistic
    D.   Kristopher and Nala, whose daughter has Down syndrome

14.16   Which of these individuals is most likely to recover poorly from a divorce?
    A.   a woman who does not remarry soon after the divorce
    B.   a woman who remarries shortly after the divorce
    C.   a man who does not remarry soon after the divorce
    D.   a man who remarries shortly after the divorce

14.17   Which of these stepparents is likely to have the easiest time establishing a
positive relationship with the stepchildren?
    A.   a stepfather with no biological children
    B.   a stepfather who has biological children
    C.   a stepmother with no biological children
    D.   a stepmother who has biological children

14.18   Partners of homosexual parents tend to be more involved with caregiving
responsibilities when
    A.   the children were adopted or conceived through reproductive
       technologies.
    B.   the children resulted from a previous heterosexual relationship.
    C.   the biological parent stays home with the children and the partner
       provides the financial support for the family.
    D.   the children are under age 5 when the relationship begins.

14.19   The most important reason for the high resignation rate for young adults is that
    A.   they have not been adequately prepared by their education.
    B.   these young people do not have a good attitude toward work.
    C.   they experience a gap between their expectations and reality.
    D.   older workers resent them and put too much pressure on them.

14.20   Research on highly gifted individuals who were followed from the 1920s found
that women in their sixties had the highest level of satisfaction with their lives if
they had
    A.   devoted themselves to their families.
    B.   pursued traditionally "feminine" jobs.
    C.   emphasized artistic self-expression.
    D.   developed rewarding careers.

Chapter 15: Practice Test

15.1   The difference in hearing loss between men and women is thought to be due to
    A.   similar factors that reduce the maximum lifespan of men.
    B.   exposure to environmental noise in male-dominated occupations.
    C.   physical damage to the eardrum due to participation in contact sports.
    D.   X-linked chromosomal abnormalities.

15.2   The inner fatty layer of the skin that softens and rounds the edges of our body is called the
    A.   epidermis.
    B.   protodermis.
    C.   dermis
    D.   hypodermis.

15.3   All of the following are benefits of hormone replacement therapy EXCEPT
    A.   protection against bone deterioration and cardiovascular disease.
    B.   an increase in hot flashes until menopause is complete.
    C.   improvement of memory and other aspects of cognition.
    D.   maintenance of cognitive functioning in late adulthood.

15.4   A man's level of the sex hormone testosterone will generally
    A.   peak in middle age, then drop off.
    B.   peak in early adulthood, then drop off.
    C.   rise steadily throughout adulthood.
    D.   remain stable throughout adulthood.

15.5   Which of these is the best description of the relationship between a couple's sexual activity and their marital happiness?
    A.   Sexual activity makes couples happier.
    B.   Being happy makes them have more sex.
    C.   It is bidirectional; each affects the other.
    D.   There is no scientific relationship between them.

15.6   Currently, the death rate from many common types of cancer is
    A.   increasing sharply.
    B.   increasing somewhat.
    C.   leveling off or dropping.
    D.   fluctuating widely.

15.7   In some individuals, indigestion-like or crushing chest pains, called _____, reveal an oxygen-deprived heart.
   A.   a heart attack
   B.   atherosclerosis
   C.   a stroke
   D.   angina pectoris

15.8   Frequent and angry outbursts; rude, disagreeable behavior; and critical and condescending nonverbal cues during social interactions are all aspects of
   A.   mental illness.
   B.   insensitivity.
   C.   competitiveness.
   D.   expressed hostility.

15.9   Sharon decided that she was unhappy at work. She realized that the primary cause was frustration with an irresponsible co-worker. She met with the individual, came up with strategies to help the young woman meet her responsibilities, and subsequently enjoyed her job more. Sharon used
   A.   Stress Identification Therapy (SIT).
   B.   an emotion-centered coping strategy.
   C.   a problem-centered coping strategy.
   D.   an indirect method of stress management.

15.10   When a person has a sense of control over life events, a commitment to important activities, and the tendency to see change as a challenge rather than a disappointment, this person is said to display
   A.   a Type A behavior pattern.
   B.   a Type B behavior pattern.
   C.   fluidity.
   D.   hardiness.

15.11   In American society, the ideal woman is portrayed as _____, and represents the heart of the double standard of aging.
   A.   passive and submissive
   B.   young and sexually attractive
   C.   indecisive and dependent
   D.   assertive and competent

15.12   Which of these tasks most clearly makes use of crystallized intelligence?
   A.   learning to speak a new language
   B.   finding hidden figures in a drawing
   C.   using the right words to express an idea
   D.   creating unusual, challenging art work

15.13 Basic information-processing skills decline throughout adulthood, but overall cognitive functioning remains quite steady. The author suggests that this apparent contradiction can be reconciled by noting that
A. adults use stronger abilities to compensate for weaker ones.
B. basic information-processing skills don't affect most abilities.
C. declines occur, but only for highly practiced, automatic skills.
D. cognitive declines are masked by social bias against older people.

15.14 The viewpoint that the general slowing of cognitive processes is due to breaks in the connections in the brain, which must then be bypassed, is called the _______ view.
A. neural network
B. information-loss
C. interconnectionist
D. path construction

15.15 As Clarissa gets older, which type of memory activity will be LESS likely to suffer?
A. matching names with faces of people she has met
B. memorization of digits such as phone numbers
C. memorization of list items
D. memorization of prose

15.16 Expertise tends to develop
A. in those who are highly educated.
B. in those at the top of administrative ladders.
C. in those from high SES backgrounds.
D. at all levels in any field of endeavor.

15.17 Research on the ability to solve everyday problems effectively shows that this ability
A. peaks about age 30 and then drops off.
B. peaks between the ages of 40 and 59.
C. doesn't reach a peak until after age 60.
D. is constant throughout adulthood.

15.18 When solving an everyday problem, middle-aged adults will do all of the following EXCEPT
A. select better strategies.
B. make decisions based on emotion.
C. solve it through logical analysis.
D. reinterpret it from a different perspective.

15.19   The impact of a challenging job on cognitive growth is greatest for
A.   individuals of any age.
B.   people in their twenties and thirties.
C.   those in administrative or supervisory positions.
D.   people living in Japan or Poland.

15.20   The most important factor in the success of an adult college student is
A.   receiving social support.
B.   a high intelligence level.
C.   taking a full course load.
D.   studying at regular times.

Chapter 16: Practice Test

16.1   At age 43, Darryl is a successful lawyer who gets a lot of satisfaction from
guiding young lawyers starting out in the firm, coaching his daughter's basketball
team, and being camp leader for his son's Boy Scout troop. According to Erikson,
he has most clearly developed a sense of
  A. intimacy.
  B. generativity.
  C. autonomy.
  D. integrity.

16.2   Although Inez has a stable marriage, three successful grown children, and a good
job, she is very self-centered and self-indulgent. She has little involvement with
her children or their families, other than to remind them what gifts she wants for
her birthday or Mother's Day. She "puts in her hours" at work, but is indifferent
to how she could improve her productivity or that of her office. Erikson would
say that Inez
  A. has developed a strong sense of stagnation.
  B. is typical of those in middle adulthood.
  C. is going through a midlife crisis.
  D. is a pain in the neck.

16.3   Which person is likely to have the largest gap between subjective and objective
age?
  A. Maria, age 25
  B. Martin, age 35
  C. Mathew, age 55
  D. MaryAnne, age 55

16.4   Which person is more likely to pursue a satisfying life structure successfully?
  A. Parker, a blue-collar worker
  B. Peter, who lives in poverty
  C. Patsanne, a corporate executive who works only the hours she wants to
  D. Penny, who is unemployed

16.5   The majority of adults experiencing a midlife transition demonstrate
  A. a sharp, sudden change in careers.
  B. a great increase in family responsibilities.
  C. major depression or anxiety attacks.
  D. small, slow changes in life structure.

16.6   Which of the following early adulthood characteristics is NOT associated with crisis during middle adulthood?
         A.   strong gender roles
         B.   low income or poverty
         C.   strong family pressures
         D.   divorce

16.7   Researchers who are proponents of the ______ approach say that middle adulthood is an adaptation to events like children growing up or an impending retirement.
         A.   stage
         B.   development
         C.   life events
         D.   social pressure

16.8   Because ______, they cannot be the single cause of midlife change.
         A.   external pressures are less during middle adulthood
         B.   life events are not as age graded as in early adulthood
         C.   changing gender roles are more common
         D.   pressures to positively impact the world occur at all age levels

16.9   As a young adult, Christian wanted to be a great athlete and a very successful businessman. As he enters middle adulthood, he will probably
         A.   strive harder to make his current self match his possible self.
         B.   become depressed that he didn't achieve his goals.
         C.   focus less on the business success and more on the athleticism in an attempt to regain his youth.
         D.   concentrate more on enhancing personal relationships and being competent at work.

16.10   In a study of well-educated individuals throughout adulthood, which of these traits showed an increase from early to middle adulthood?
         A.   insecurity
         B.   depression
         C.   self-acceptance
         D.   isolation

16.11   Shakira, an office supervisor, is well liked and respected by those who work for her. She can find the "silver lining" to a stressful situation, anticipates and plans for possible problems, and uses humor to express ideas and feelings. Shakira is probably
         A.   a middle-aged individual.
         B.   not effective as a supervisor, even though she is well liked.
         C.   using emotion-centered strategies for coping with stress.
         D.   a young adult.

16.12 Warren is generous, kind, and good-natured. He always has good words to say about his friends and tries to find the best qualities in everyone he meets. Warren best exemplifies which of these "big five" personality traits?
A. extroversion
B. conscientiousness
C. agreeableness
D. neuroticism

16.13 The modern view of the period between the departure of the last child and retirement is viewed as a time of
A. expansion and new horizons.
B. sadness and the "empty nest."
C. increasing marital stress.
D. isolation from social activities.

16.14 Your friend's children will be growing up and leaving home in the next five years or so, and your friend is concerned about how satisfying life can be after they are gone. According to the book, the best advice you can give for ensuring increased life happiness after they leave is for her to
A. develop a strong work orientation.
B. spend as much time with them as possible now.
C. keep them in the family unit as long as possible.
D. separate completely from them after they go.

16.15 Middle-aged adults who balance the needs of aging parents and financially dependent children are called
A. real troopers.
B. kinkeepers.
C. economically challenged.
D. the sandwich generation.

16.16 Which event tends to cause an increase in sibling ties during middle adulthood?
A. the birth of children
B. beginning a new job
C. the birth of grandchildren
D. parental illness

16.17 Eighteen-year-old Tim believes that government programs for the elderly are too costly. Which of the following activities could increase his endorsement of these benefits?
A. education on the tax structure of the United States
B. increased awareness of health care costs for elderly adults
C. frequent contact with his grandparents
D. eventually becoming a senior citizen himself

16.18   Which aspect of a worker's job satisfaction changes the most during adulthood?
        A.   intrinsic satisfaction
        B.   extrinsic satisfaction
        C.   borderline satisfaction
        D.   corporate satisfaction

16.19   The most important factor in helping middle-aged workers cope with losing their jobs is
        A.   leaving them alone to preserve their dignity.
        B.   social contact with those who share their values.
        C.   getting them involved with household management.
        D.   pretending that nothing has really changed.

16.20   Retirement can be stressful since it leads to a loss of two important work-related rewards,
        A.   income and benefits.
        B.   interaction with others and a steady income.
        C.   income and status.
        D.   intrinsic and extrinsic satisfaction.

Chapter 17: Practice Test

17.1   Charlie, at age 82, is vigorous, healthy, and looks younger than he really is. Charlie would be classified as
        A.   immature.
        B.   postmature.
        C.   old-old.
        D.   young-old.

17.2   The percentage of elderly people in the population of the United States is lower than in many other industrialized nations due in part to
        A.   particularly strong strains of influenza during the last five years.
        B.   low birthrates among America's poverty-stricken groups.
        C.   less effective public policies ensuring health and well-being throughout the lifespan.
        D.   zero population growth during the last decade.

17.3   Ellen is worried about developing macular degeneration. What can she do to reduce her risk of acquiring this condition?
        A.   avoid reading, as it strains the eyes
        B.   wear bifocals
        C.   eat lots of spinach
        D.   wear reading glasses

17.4   Compared with vision loss in elderly people, hearing loss has a larger effect on a person's
        A.   safety and enjoyment of life.
        B.   ability to live independently.
        C.   self-esteem.
        D.   employment.

17.5   An important reason elderly people become more out of breath while exercising than younger adults do is that
        A.   their hearts pump blood more quickly.
        B.   their lungs fill and empty less effectively.
        C.   their brains demand more oxygen.
        D.   their muscles demand more oxygen.

17.6   All of the following contribute to a higher incidence of sleep disturbances in men than in women EXCEPT
        A.   sleep apnea.
        B.   enlargement of the prostate gland.
        C.   restless legs.
        D.   lower levels of both testosterone and estrogen.

17.7   Weight changes after age 60 typically involve
        A.   less fat accumulated on the torso.
        B.   weight gain due to decreased activity.
        C.   weight loss due to less lean body mass.
        D.   weight gain from fat accumulations.

17.8   In several studies, 12 to 20 percent of elders with disabilities
        A.   died within 2 years of becoming disabled.
        B.   showed improvement 2 to 6 years later.
        C.   maintained their independent living status with no outside support from
             others.
        D.   had become disabled due to injuries that occurred during early
             adulthood that had not been treated properly.

17.9   Your elderly neighbor is wondering whether or not to take a vitamin-mineral
        nutritional supplement. What advice should you give?
        A.   There is no evidence that supplements make any difference.
        B.   Vitamin supplements are not necessary if you are eating well.
        C.   These supplements are only useful for very active people.
        D.   These supplements have proven benefits for most elders.

17.10   Which of these is the best example of primary aging?
        A.   far-sightedness from a stiffening lens
        B.   lung cancer from smoking cigarettes
        C.   weight gain from a sedentary lifestyle
        D.   high blood pressure from prolonged stress

17.11   An autoimmune response that leads to inflammation of connective tissue and
        subsequent overall stiffness, inflammation, and aching is called
        A.   osteoarthritis.
        B.   adult-onset diabetes.
        C.   rheumatoid arthritis.
        D.   bursitis.

17.12   At which age is the death rate from unintentional injuries highest?
        A.   middle adulthood
        B.   adolescence
        C.   late adulthood
        D.   young adulthood

17.13   The most common form of dementia is
        A.   cerebrovascular dementia.
        B.   cardiovascular disease.
        C.   Alzheimer's disease.
        D.   retrograde amnesia.

17.14   Bundles of twisted threads inside neurons that are the product of collapsed
        neural structures are called
            A.   amyloid plaques.
            B.   cerebrovascular bundles.
            C.   neurofibrillary tangles.
            D.   brain breaks.

17.15   Which person is MOST likely to be placed in a nursing home?
            A.   Neva, an 83-year-old African-American
            B.   Natasha, an 80-year-old Caucasian-American
            C.   Nyree, a 90-year-old Japanese great-grandmother
            D.   Nyung, a 95-year-old Asian-American

17.16   When older adults engage in selective optimization with compensation, they
            A.   select only activities that are personally valued to optimize their energy
                 and they also develop ways to compensate for losses.
            B.   tend to show gains in fluid intelligence.
            C.   show losses in crystallized intelligence only.
            D.   attend to only certain parts of a conversation (selective optimization)
                 and then try to fill in the missing pieces later (compensation).

17.17   Which of these language abilities remains the most constant as adults grow
        older?
            A.   retrieving words from long-term memory
            B.   language comprehension
            C.   planning and organizing speech
            D.   inventing new words and phrases

17.18   According to your text, wisdom can be summed up as
            A.   a cumulative benefit of age.
            B.   expertise in the fundamental pragmatics of life.
            C.   an intrinsic characteristic that develops with age.
            D.   general familiarity with human problems.

17.19   A steady, marked decrease in cognitive functions shortly before death is referred
        to as
            A.   increased morbidity.
            B.   the cognitive slope.
            C.   mental despair.
            D.   terminal decline.

17.20   One serious drawback to the Elderhostel program is that
            A.   it is not accessible to low-SES people.
            B.   it gives elders a false sense of importance.
            C.   there is no screening for the program's teachers.
            D.   most programs are too demanding physically.

Chapter 18: Practice Test

18.1   According to Erikson, developing a sense of ego integrity depends on
     A.   viewing one's life in the context of all of humanity.
     B.   the willingness to open up one's life to another person.
     C.   deciding who one is and what one wants from life.
     D.   the desire to make a contribution to the next generation.

18.2   Yin-sing, at age 80, can't face the idea that she will die and the world will go on. She has children and grandchildren, but is not interested in their lives or fortunes. According to Peck, Yin-sing needs to work on
     A.   body transcendence.
     B.   ego transcendence.
     C.   ego differentiation.
     D.   future differentiation.

18.3   When asked, approximately one-third of elders claimed that the best part of their life was _____, thus _____ the belief that older adults wish to be young again.
     A.   childhood; verifying
     B.   "right now"; contradicting
     C.   young adulthood; verifying
     D.   "still to come"; contradicting

18.4   Which of these personality traits tends to DECREASE as adults grow old?
     A.   Agreeableness
     B.   Acceptance of change
     C.   Sociability
     D.   Satisfaction

18.5   Because Mahatma Gandhi and Martin Luther Ling, Jr., stood up against persecution and injustice in order to promote their visions of an all-inclusive human community, they had attained which of Fowler's stages of faith development?
     A.   synthetic-conventional
     B.   conjunctive
     C.   individuative-reflective
     D.   intuitive-projective

18.6   Because of the gender-related life changes in very old age, women are more likely to report _____ than are men.
     A.   a higher sense of psychological well-being
     B.   a lower sense of psychological well-being
     C.   more dependence on others
     D.   more frequent thoughts of suicide

18.7	Ethnic minority elders who are offered formal agency services to help with their lives will generally
        A.   accept formal agency services quite readily.
        B.   resist unless the agencies are culturally sensitive.
        C.   resist all types of formal agency services.
        D.   accept only formal services that are family based.

18.8	According to the ______, when society arranges conditions that permit elders to remain engaged in roles and relationships, life satisfaction is improved and social interactions increase.
        A.   mutuality theory
        B.   activity theory
        C.   socioemotional selectivity theory
        D.   disengagement theory

18.9	Although the social networks of older adults are ______, they report being ______ than younger adults with their current number of friends.
        A.   larger; more dissatisfied
        B.   larger; happier
        C.   smaller; happier
        D.   smaller; more dissatisfied

18.10	Which of the following is the primary reason that elders residing in small and mid-sized communities are more satisfied with life?
        A.   children tend to live closer
        B.   more opportunities for interaction with others of the same ethnic background
        C.   higher participation in local government
        D.   lower crime rates

18.11	Although increasing numbers of ethnic minority elders want to live on their own, ______ prevent(s) them from doing so.
        A.   pride
        B.   cultural values
        C.   their children
        D.   poverty

18.12	An elder's autonomy is restricted most sharply if he or she is living in
        A.   his or her own home.
        B.   a nursing home.
        C.   congregate housing.
        D.   an adult child's home.

18.13   The increase in marital satisfaction in late adulthood is due to all of the
following EXCEPT
     A.   increased perceptions of fairness as men contribute more to household
tasks.
     B.   engagement in more joint leisure activities.
     C.   greater financial security.
     D.   more positive interactions due to greater emotional understanding.

18.14   Compared with younger adults, elders who must cope with the death of a spouse
typically show
     A.   the same type and intensity of reactions.
     B.   a less intense but longer-lasting reaction.
     C.   more problems adjusting to the death.
     D.   fewer problems adjusting to the death.

18.15   Elderly women who are asked to list the functions of close friendships in their
lives give primary importance to
     A.   living assistance.
     B.   acceptance.
     C.   links to the outside world.
     D.   companionship.

18.16   The kind of assistance that elders expect from their adult children most often
involves
     A.   help with day-to-day living tasks.
     B.   advice and emotional support.
     C.   financial assistance with living expenses.
     D.   help in dealing with medical emergencies.

18.17   Elder abuse is more common if the elder's caregiver is
     A.   a sibling or other close relative of the elder.
     B.   an adult who is at least middle-aged or older.
     C.   emotionally or financially dependent on the elder.
     D.   working in a challenging, rewarding career.

18.18   Women are more likely to retire earlier than men because
     A.   they are typically better off financially.
     B.   they tend to be in better health.
     C.   they work in unstimulating environments.
     D.   of family events.

18.19   Miguel works for a community center and wants to recruit elders as volunteers
        for an after-school reading program. Which of the following people is NOT a
        likely candidate?
            A. Carl, a lifelong community activist and volunteer
            B. Marcos, who has never volunteered and retired 4 years ago
            C. Maria, who has never volunteered for anything and retired 6 months
                ago
            D. Reuben, a highly educated and financially secure elder

18.20   Modern definitions of successful aging have shifted the focus AWAY from
            A. specific achievements in health or cognitive functioning.
            B. the processes elders use to reach personally valued goals.
            C. accepting and learning to compensate for personal declines.
            D. the ways in which elders minimize losses and maximize gains.

Chapter 19: Practice Test

19.1   Death is long and drawn out for _____ of people due to _____.
        A.   only a small percentage; life-saving medical technology
        B.   only a small percentage; the increasing popularity of living wills
        C.   three-fourths; life-saving medical technology
        D.   nearly 90 percent; increases in diseases like cancer and AIDS

19.2   Brianna was found unconscious in a swimming pool. Her heartbeat and breathing had stopped, and her dilated pupils indicated lack of oxygen to her brain. Yet, paramedics were able to revive her. Brianna was in the _____ phase of dying.
        A.   agonal
        B.   clinical
        C.   mortality
        D.   miracle

19.3   The term used by the medical profession for individuals whose brain stems continue to function but who show no electrical activity at all in the cortex is
        A.   brain death.
        B.   persistent vegetative state.
        C.   imminent mortality.
        D.   coma.

19.4   Karim has grown up in the United States, in a suburban neighborhood. As a result, he is probably _____ death.
        A.   comfortable with
        B.   used to dealing with
        C.   very familiar with
        D.   insulated from

19.5   Which of these aspects of the death concept is most difficult for children to comprehend?
        A.   Dead people no longer eat, breathe, or move.
        B.   Dead people will not wake up or come alive again.
        C.   Dead people cannot think, feel, or understand.
        D.   All people will die at some time or other.

19.6   Among elders in Western cultures such as the United States, the most important factor in reducing death anxiety is
        A.   a spiritual sense of life's meaning.
        B.   commitment to an organized religion.
        C.   the conviction that there is an afterlife.
        D.   good physical health for one's age.

19.7   When going through Kübler-Ross's phases of dying, people
   A.   move through each stage in a sequential manner.
   B.   move back and forth between stages.
   C.   often linger at the anger stage and must be pushed to the next stage by family or health care professionals.
   D.   rarely progress to the acceptance stage.

19.8   According to Kübler-Ross, once a dying patient has reached the stage of acceptance he or she will often
   A.   appear cheerful and eager for death.
   B.   become more sociable and outgoing.
   C.   feel no hope at all of avoiding death.
   D.   withdraw from most or all people.

19.9   _____ is an alternative to Kübler-Ross's stages that theorists say makes sense in terms of the individual's pattern of living and values, preserves or restores significant relationships, and is as free of suffering as possible.
   A.   Passive euthanasia
   B.   Voluntary active euthanasia
   C.   Assisted suicide
   D.   An appropriate death

19.10   The primary reason some caregivers join in a dying patient's denial by pretending that they will get better and continue to live is that
   A.   the patient seems so healthy they forget he or she is dying.
   B.   the patient becomes too angry whenever dying is mentioned.
   C.   it is difficult to face the impending death and to close off relationships.
   D.   they don't want to be bothered with discussing death.

19.11   When a dying person feels a strong sense of spirituality, it tends to produce
   A.   less fear of death and more acceptance of dying.
   B.   more anger at a God who should have prevented this.
   C.   confusion and distress at what dying really means.
   D.   anger and resentment at those who go on living.

19.12   In the United States today, passive euthanasia for patients whose death is imminent or who are in a permanent coma is considered
   A.   an ordinary part of normal medical practice.
   B.   an unusual procedure that must be court ordered.
   C.   immoral and unethical and almost never occurs.
   D.   permissible only for patients who are very old.

19.13   _____ is a written statement of desired medical treatment should a person become incurably ill. Two types are recognized in most states.
   A.   An advance medical directive
   B.   A living will
   C.   Durable power of attorney for health care
   D.   A codicil

19.14   The durable power of attorney for medical care is particularly useful for ensuring the partner's role
   A.   in states in which euthanasia is illegal.
   B.   in situations other than terminal illness.
   C.   in relationships not recognized or sanctioned by law.
   D.   when mental as well as physical difficulties are present.

19.15   A central philosophy of the _____ is that the dying person and his or her family should be offered choices that guarantee an appropriate death.
   A.   home-choice
   B.   intensive care unit
   C.   hospice approach
   D.   emergency room procedure

19.16   After Jada's sister died, she experienced intense physical and psychological distress. Jada was experiencing
   A.   bereavement.
   B.   grief.
   C.   a near-death experience.
   D.   mourning.

19.17   Many of the reactions of the confrontation phase—such as anxiety, anger, frustration, sleeplessness and loss of appetite—are symptoms of
   A.   depression, an invariable component of grieving.
   B.   avoidance.
   C.   mourning, a necessary phase of grieving.
   D.   poor coping strategies.

19.18   During the accommodation phase of the grieving process, a bereaved person's focus shifts to
   A.   a strong yearning or desire to be with the deceased again.
   B.   anger at those who survived when the loved one didn't.
   C.   putting the deceased in the past and forgetting him or her.
   D.   the surrounding world and going on with one's life.

19.19   Parents of children who have close family members who are dying would be
         best advised to
                A.   remove the children from the household until the death is over.
                B.   be honest about what is happening and answer their questions.
                C.   keep the truth from them as long as possible so they won't worry.
                D.   use comforting phrases such as "he's going to be with the angels."

19.20   Research indicates that the LEAST effective method of providing death
         education is
                A.   a program to help students confront their own mortality.
                B.   discussions with terminally ill patients and their families.
                C.   visits to mortuaries, cemeteries, and funeral homes.
                D.   lectures giving factual information about the dying process.

Chapter 1: Answers

1.1   D   A theory's continued existence depends on scientific verification. This means that the they must be tested with a fair set of research procedures agreed on by the scientific community, and its findings must endure over time. p. 7

1.2   A   A psychologist who assumes that there are many courses of development would most likely emphasize that children live in distinct contexts and experience unique combinations of biological and environmental circumstances. p. 7

1.3   C   The lifespan perspective regards the challenges and adjustments of development as multidimensional – affected by an intricate blend of biological, psychological, and social forces. p. 9

1.4   A   Lifespan researchers emphasize that development is highly plastic, or open to change in response to diverse life events, at all ages. p. 10

1.5   C   In medieval times, there were no philosophies of the uniqueness of childhood or separate developmental periods. Once children emerged from infancy, they were regarded as miniature, already formed adults. p. 13

1.6   D   Darwin's efforts to chart parallels between child growth and human evolution prompted researchers to make careful observations of all aspects of children's behavior. Out of these first attempts to document ideas about development, scientific child study was born. p. 14

1.7   C   In the psychoanalytic approach, people move through a series of stages in which they confront conflicts between biological drives and social expectations. The way these conflicts are resolved influences development. p. 16

1.8   B   According to behaviorism, the proper focus of the study of psychology should be directly observable events – stimuli and responses. p. 18

1.9   A   Like Piaget's cognitive-developmental theory, information processing regards people as active, sense-making beings who modify their own thinking in response to environmental demands. p. 20

1.10 D   Unlike Piaget, Vygotksy viewed development as a socially mediated process – as dependent on the support that adults and more mature peers provide as children try new tasks. p. 24

1.11   B   Bronfenbrenner expanded the view of the environment by envisioning it as a series of nested structures that includes but extends beyond the home, school, neighborhood, and workplace settings in which people spend their everyday lives. pp. 25-26

1.12   D   The great strength of naturalistic observation is that investigators can see directly the everyday behaviors they hope to explain. p. 29

1.13   D   The ethnographic approach assumes that by becoming part of the cultural community, researchers can understand the beliefs and behavior of its members more accurately, in a way not possible with an observational visit, interview, or questionnaire. p. 30

1.14   C   The correlational design offers a way of looking at relationships between the participants' experiences or characteristics and their behavior or development. Correlational studies cannot infer cause and effect. p. 32

1.15   C   Inferences about cause-and-effect relationships are possible in experiments because the researcher directly controls or manipulates changes in the independent variable. p. 34

1.16   A   Random assignment is an evenhanded procedure for assigning participants to treatment groups, such as flipping a coin. p. 34

1.17   D   Findings obtained in laboratory experiments may not always apply to everyday situations. The ideal solution to this problem is to do experiments in the field as a complement to laboratory investigations. p. 34

1.18   A   In longitudinal research, participants may move away or drop out, changing the makeup of the original sample. Participants' performance may improve as a result of practice effects, not because of factors associated with development. Cohort effects limit the generalizability of findings to individuals born in the same time period. p. 37

1.19   D   In cross-sectional research, evidence about change at the level at which it actually occurs – the individual – is not available. p. 38

1.20   C   Ethical standards permit deception if investigators satisfy institutional committees that such practices are necessary. p. 40

Chapter 2: Answers

2.1   A   Chromosomes are rodlike structures in the cell nucleus that store and transmit genetic information. p. 46

2.2   A   Mitosis refers to the process of cell duplication through which each new body cell receives an exact copy of the original chromosomes. Meiosis refers to the process of cell division through which gametes are formed and in which the number of chromosomes in each cell is halved. p. 47

2.3   D   A gamete, or sex cell, contains 23 chromosomes, half as many as a regular body cell. When sperm and ovum unite at conception, the cell that results, called a zygote, will have 46 chromosomes. p. 47

2.4   D   In males, the 23rd pair of chromosomes, or sex chromosomes, is called XY; in females it is called XX. p. 48

2.5   D   Fraternal, or dizygotic twins are created when two different eggs are fertilized.Identical, or monozygotic twins are formed when a zygote separates into two clusters of cells that develop into two individuals. p. 48

2.6   A   If the genes from both parents are alike, the child is homozygous; if they are different, the child is heterozygous. In dominant-recessive inheritance, a recessive gene is not expressed in the presence of a dominant gene. Symbolizing a dominant gene by a capital D and a recessive genes by a lower case d, DD represents an example of dominant homozygous, dd recessive homozygous, and Dd dominant heterozygous. p. 49

2.7   D   PKU, or phenylketonuria, provides an example of howchanges in the environment can alter the extent to which an inherited disorder influences a person's well-being. If the disease is found in a newborn, the infant can be placed on a diet low in phenylalanine and expect to have a normal lifespan and attain average intelligence. p. 49

2.8   C   When a harmful gene is carried on the X chromosome, males, with XY sex chromosomes, are more likely than females, with XX sex chromosomes, to be affected by the disorder. In females, any recessive gene on one X has a good chance of being suppressed by a dominant gene on the other X. The Y chromosome is only about one-third as long and therefore lacks many corresponding genes to override those on the X. pp. 51-52

2.9   A   Characteristics that vary continuously among people, such as height, musical ability, or intelligence, are most likely determined by polygenic inheritance, in which many genes determine the characteristic in question. p. 53

2.10   C   Verbal difficulties (for example, with reading and vocabulary) are common among girls with triple X syndrome (XXX) and boys with Klinefelter syndrome (XXY), both of whom inherit an extra X chromosome. p. 54

2.11   B   Prenatal diagnostic methods other than maternal blood analysis and ultrasound, such as amniocentesis, chorionic villus sampling, and fetoscopy entail some risk of miscarriage. Also, chorionic villus sampling is associated with a small risk of limb deformities. p. 58

2.12   C   According to Bronfenbrenner's ecological systems theory, all relationships within the family are bidirectional – the behaviors of each family member affect those of others. p. 62

2.13   B   Since the 1970s, the child poverty rate in the United States has been higher than that of any other age group. p. 64

2.14   D   Compared to large urban areas, in small towns connections between settings that influence children's lives, such as teachers and parents, are more common. p. 66

2.15   D   The United States is among the wealthiest of nations and has the broadest knowledge base for intervening effectively in children's lives. However, American public policies safeguarding children have been slower to emerge than in other Western industrialized nations. p. 68

2.16   A   The United Sates ranks 20th worldwide in terms of the percent of low-birth-weight newborns. The United States trails Kuwait, Egypt, and Romania. p. 68

2.17   B   A concordance rate ranges from 0 to 100 percent. A score of 0 indicates that if one twin has the trait, the other one never has it, whereas score of 100 means that if one twin has the trait, the other one always has it. Therefore, a concordance rate of 75 percent indicates that if one twin has the trait, the other one will have it three-quarters of the time. p. 72

2.18   D   Heritability estimates and concordance rates measure the extent to which individual differences in complex traits in a specific population are due to genetic factors. The remaining variation is explained by individual differences in environmental influences. pp. 72-73

2.19   C   Canalization refers to the tendency of heredity to restrict the development of some characteristics to just one or a few outcomes. A behavior that is strongly canalized follows a genetically set growth plan, and only powerful environmental forces can change it. p. 74

2.20   A   According to the concept of genetic-environmental correlation, our genes
            influence the environment to which we are exposed. The findings of this
            study show that heredity played some role in influencing the adolescents'
            parenting. p. 74

Chapter 3: Answers

3.1   B   During the period of the embryo, the ectoderm folds over to form a neural tube, which will become the spinal cord and brain. p. 83

3.2   B   The point at which a fetus can first survive, called the age of viability, occurs sometime between 22 and 26 weeks. p. 84

3.3   D   In the period of the zygote, before implantation, teratogens rarely have any impact. If they do, the zygote is so completely damaged it dies. During the fetal period, damage by teratogens is usually minor. The embryonic period is the time when serious defects are most likely to occur, since the foundation for all body parts are laid down. p. 87

3.4   C   Nicotine, the addictive substance in tobacco, causes the placenta to grow abnormally. Also, smoking raises the concentration of carbon monoxide in the bloodstreams of both mother and fetus. Carbon monoxide displaces oxygen from red blood cells. p. 90

3.5   B   Fetal alcohol syndrome (FAS) results when women consume large amount of alcohol during most of all of pregnancy. Mothers of children with fetal alcohol effects (FAE) usually drink alcohol in smaller quantities than did mothers of children with FAS. p. 91

3.6   C   Folic acid supplementation around the time of conception reduces neural tube defects by as much as 72 percent. Adequate folate intake during the last 10 weeks of pregnancy cuts the risk of premature delivery and low birth weight in half. p. 93

3.7   D   Severe emotional stress during pregnancy reduces blood flow to the uterus. As a result, the fetus receives less oxygen and nutrients. p. 94

3.8   A   Pregnant women who wait until after the first trimester to seek prenatal care or never get any at all are far more likely to have infants born underweight and infants whodie before birth or during the first year of life. p. 95

3.9   D   During the third stage of labor, labor comes to an end with a few final contractions and pushes that cause the placenta to separate from the wall of the uterus and be delivered. p. 97

3.10 B The force of the contractions causes infants to produce high levels of stress hormones during childbirth. Infants' production of stress hormones during delivery is adaptive because it prepares newborns to breathe effectively by causing the lungs to absorb excess liquid and by expanding the bronchial tubes. p. 98

3.11 C The Apgar Scale rates newborns on each of five characteristics from 0 to 2 at 1 and 5 minutes after birth. An Apgar score of 7 or better indicates that the infant is in good physical condition. pp. 98-99

3.12 C For healthy women who are assisted by a well-trained doctor or midwife, home delivery is safe, since complications rarely occur. p. 100

3.13 B Fetal monitoring has saved the lives of many high-risk babies. In healthy pregnancies, it does not reduce the rate of infant brain damage or death. Monitoring is linked to an increased rate of cesarean deliveries. p. 101

3.14 D The cesarean rate in the United States in 1998 was 21 percent of births – the highest rate in the world. p. 101

3.15 B Only small-for-date infants likely experienced inadequate prenatal nutrition. Perhaps their mothers did not eat properly, the placenta did not function properly, or the babies themselves had defects that prevented them from growing as they should. p. 102

3.16 D Reflexes provide pediatricians one way of assessing the health of the baby's nervous system. Weak or absent reflexes, reflexes that are overly rigid or exaggerated, and reflexes that persist beyond the point in development in which they should normally disappear can signal brain damage. p. 106

3.17 C The infant's breathing is even in both quiet alertness and regular sleep. In the other states of arousal, breathing is irregular. p. 108

3.18 A Infants spend more time in REM sleep than do children and adults. REM sleep accounts for 50 percent of a newborn's sleep time. By 3 to 5 years, it has declined to an adultlike 20 percent. p. 108

3.19 A Bottle-fed babies orient to the smell of any lactating woman over the smells of formula or a nonlactating woman. p. 110

3.20 B NBAS "recovery curves" predict intelligence with moderate success well into the preschool years. p. 111

Chapter 4: Answers

4.1   D   At birth, the skeletal age of girls is about 4 to 6 weeks ahead of that of boys. This gap widens over infancy and childhood, with girls reaching their full body size several years before boys. p. 119

4.2   A   During prenatal development, the head develops more rapidly than the lower part of the body. This developmental trend is referred to as the cephalocaudal trend, meaning "head to tail" in Latin. p. 120

4.3   D   Synaptic pruning is the process by which seldom-stimulated neurons are returned to an uncommitted state so they can support the development of future skills. For this process to go forward, appropriate stimulation of the brain is vital when the formation of synapses is at its peak. p. 120

4.4   A   Glial cells are responsible for the dramatic increase in brain size during the first two years. They are responsible for myelinization and multiply dramatically from the fourth month of pregnancy through the second year of life. p. 121

4.5   C   Once the two hemispheres lateralize, the cortex is no longer higher plastic--damage to a particular region means that the abilities controlled by it will be lost forever. p. 122

4.6   C   Trying to prime infants with stimulation for which they are not ready--as in these early learning centers--can cause them to withdraw. Their interest in learning may be threatened and they may act much like stimulus-deprived infants. p. 124

4.7   D   Through breast-feeding, antibodies and other infection-fighting agents are transferred from mother to child. As a result, breast-fed babies have far fewer illnesses and allergies than do bottle-fed infants. p. 127

4.8   A   Improving marasmic chidren's diets leads to some catch-up growth in height, but little improvement in head size. The malnutrition probably interferes with growth of neural fibers and myelinization, causing a permanent loss in brain weight. p. 128

4.9   A   Nonorganic failure to thrive is a growth disorder usually present by 18 months that is caused by lack of affection and stimulation. Infants who have it show no organic cause for a failure to grow. p. 129

4.11   C   This is an example of operant conditioning. The behavior of each partner reinforces the other, and as a result, both parent and baby continue their pleasurable interaction. p. 131

4.12   A   Habituation is the process whereby a repetitive stimulus becomes so familiar that the responses initially associated with it (for example, looking) no longer occur. This method does not provide information about infants' preferences. p. 131

4.13   B   Newborn imitation is flexible and voluntary because newborns imitate many facial expressions after short delays. p. 132

4.14   B   This is an example of the proximodistal trend, which refers to the pattern of physical growth and motor control than proceeds from the center of the body outward. p. 134

4.15   D   The sequence of motor development is fairly uniform across children, although there are large individual differences in the rate of motor progress. Parents should be concerned about their child's development only if many motor skills are seriously delayed. p. 134

4.16   D   Among the Kipsigis of Kenya, babies hold their heads up, sit alone, and walk considerably earlier than North American infants. Kipsigi parents deliberately teach these motor skills. p. 134

4.17   A   Around 3 months, infants reach just as effectively for a sounding object in the dark as for an object in the light. From the start, vision is freed from the basic action of reaching so it can focus on more complex adjustments. p. 135

4.18   B   If babies are sensitive to the contrast in two or more patterns, they prefer to look at stimuli with the most contrast, such as a black-and-white drawing. Also, because of their poor vision, very young babies cannot resolve the features in more complex patterns, such as a checkerboard with many squares. p. 140

4.19   A   Research suggests that intermodal perception is present at birth. Newborns turn in the general direction of a sound and reach for objects in a primitive way. p. 142

4.20   D   According to differentiation theory, infants actively search for invariant features of the environment—those that remain stable—in a constantly changing world. This capacity to search for order and consistency becomes more fine-tuned with age. pp. 142-143

Chapter 5: Answers

5.1   C   Schemes move from an action-based level to a mental level with the transition from sensorimotor to preoperational thought. p. 148

5.2   B   During rapid cognitive change, children are in a state of disequilibrium. They realize that new information does not match their current schemes, so they shift away from assimilation toward accommodation. p. 149

5.3   C   Using the secondary circular reaction, infants try to repeat interesting events caused by their own actions. p. 150

5.4   D   During Substage 4 in the sensorimotor period, infants start to combine secondary circular reaction into new, more complex action sequences. The ability to engage in intentional, or goal-directed, behavior and the attainment of object permanence are two resulting landmark cognitive changes. p. 151

5.5   A   Recent research suggests that babies who do not try to search for hidden objects cannot yet put together the separate schemes to retrieve a hidden toy, such as pushing aside the obstacle and grasping the object. p. 153

5.6   D   Recent research on sensorimotor development has shown that infants comprehend a great deal about the world before they are capable of the motor behaviors Piaget assumed were responsible for those understandings. p. 155

5.7   C   Although gains in information-processing capacity are partly due to brain development, they are largely the result of improvements in mental strategies, such as attending to information and categorizing it effectively. p. 157

5.8   B   Habituation-dishabituation research indicates that babies seem to remember best when experiences take place in familiar contexts and when they participate actively. p. 157

5.9   D   For memories to become autobiographical, the child must have a well-developed image of the self and must be able to integrate personal experiences into a meaningful life story. p. 159

5.10 C   According to Vygotsky, the zone of proximal development refers to a range of tasks that the child cannot yet handle alone but can do with the help of more skilled partners. p. 160

5.11 B   Because infant intelligence tests show better long-term prediction for extremely low-scoring babies, they are used largely for helping to identify infants whose very low scores mean that they are likely to have developmental problems in the future. p. 163

5.12 D   The habituation-dishabituation response may be a more effective predictor of later IQ than traditional infant tests because it assesses quickness of thinking, a characteristic of bright individuals. p. 163

5.13 A   High Home Observations for Measurement of the Environment (HOME) scores are associated with IQ gains between 1 and 3 years of age. p. 163

5.14 B   Child care standards are set by the states, and some do not require caregivers to have special training in child development. p. 164

5.15 A   By 12 months of age, the IQs of control and treatment children diverged. The treatment children maintained their IQ advantage well into adolescence. p. 166

5.16 D   In a nativist account, all children are born with a language acquisition device (LAD), a biologically based innate set of rules common to all languages. It permits children to understand and speak in a rule-oriented fashion as soon as they have picked up enough words. p. 167

5.17 D   Research on babbling shows that babies everywhere start babbling at about the same age and produce a similar range of early sounds. But for babbling to develop further, infants must be able to hear human speech sounds. If hearing is impaired, babbling is greatly delayed. p. 168

5.18 A   This is an example of an underextension--an early vocabulary error in which a word is applied too narrowly, to a smaller number of objects or events than is appropriate. p. 169

5.19 C   Research shows that children with an expressive language style, who believe that words are for talking about people's feelings and needs, often are engaged in social routines by their families. p. 170

5.20 A   Conversational give-and-take between parent and toddler is one of the best predictors of early language development and academic competence during the school years. p. 172

Chapter 6: Answers

6.1 C Warm, responsive caregiving leads infants to resolve the psychological conflict of basic trust versus mistrust on the positive side. p. 178

6.2 D During the first 2 months, fleeting expressions of anger appear as babies cry. From 4 to 6 months into the second year, older babies show anger in a wider range of situations, such as when an object is taken away. p. 182

6.3 D Social referencing is relying on another person's emotional reaction to appraise an uncertain situation. p. 183

6.4 A Self-conscious emotions, such as shame, guilt, and pride, appear between 18 and 24 months, as the sense of self emerges. p. 183

6.5 A Emotional self-regulation involves the strategies we use to adjust our emotional state to a comfortable level of intensity so we can accomplish our goals. Each of the examples, except for the child who feels proud of getting good grades, deals with attempts to regulate emotional states. p. 184

6.6 A Thomas and Chess found that temperament is not fixed and unchangeable. Parenting practices can modify children's emotional styles considerably. p. 185

6.7 C Compared to sociable, uninhibited children, shy, inhibited children show greater right than left frontal brain wave activity and greater pupil dilation and a drop in blood pressure in response to novelty. Salivary cortisol tends to be higher in shy than sociable children. p. 186

6.8 B Infants who score low or high on attention span, activity level, irritability, sociability, or shyness are likely to respond similarly when assessed again several months to a few years later. p. 188

6.9 B Rather than assuming that each child shares the same temperament, parents often look for and emphasize each child's unique characteristics. For example, when one child in a family is perceived as easy, another is likely to be regarded as difficult, even though the second child might not be very difficult when compared to children in general. p. 189

6.10 C In a famous experiment by Harlow, rhesus monkeys reared with terrycloth and wire-mesh "surrogate mothers" clung to the soft terrycloth substitute, even though the wire-mesh "mother" held the bottle and infants had to climb on it to be fed. p. 190

6.11   D   Infants in the phase of clearcut attachment, which lasts from 6 to 8 months to
             18 to 24 months, babies display separation anxiety, becoming upset when the
             familiar caregiver leaves. p. 191

6.12   C   During the Strange Situation, when the parent leaves for a brief time, the
             child should show separation anxiety. When the parent returns, the child
             should actively seek contact and his or her crying should be reduced
             immediately. p. 191

6.13   D   Rutter's study of institutionalized infants indicates that fully normal
             development depends on establishing close bonds with caregivers during the
             first few years of life. Children who developed their first attachment bond
             after toddlerhood were more likely to display social and emotional problems.
             p. 193

6.14   C   Emmanuel's behavior pattern during the Strange Situation is characteristic of
             resistant babies, who often experience inconsistent care. Their mothers are
             often unresponsive to infant signals. Yet when the baby begins to explore,
             they interfere, shifting the infant's attention back to themselves. As a result,
             the baby is overly dependent and angry at the mother's lack of involvement.
             p. 6.22

6.15   C   The way parents view their childhoods--their ability to include new
             information in their working models, to come to terms with negative life
             events, and to look back on their own parents in an understanding, forgiving
             way--is much more influential in how they care for their children than the
             actual history of care they received. p. 194

6.16   D   Mothers more often engage in conventional games such as pat-a-cake and
             peekaboo. In contrast, fathers tend to engage in more exciting, highly
             physical bouncing and lifting games. p. 195

6.17   B   Mothers are more positive and playful with second-borns than first-borns--
             behaviors that can spark feelings of rivalry and behavior problems in the
             older child. p. 197

6.18   C   In the NICHD Study of Early Child Care, when babies were exposed to
             combined home and child-care risk factors--insensitive caregiving at home
             with insensitive caregiving in child care, long hours in child care, or more
             than one child-care arrangement--the rate of insecurity increased. p. 196

6.19   A   The I-self is a sense of self as subject, or agent, who is separate from but
             attends to and acts on objects and other people. p. 199

6.20   C   The beginnings of self-control appear as compliance. Between 12 and 18
            months, children show clear awareness of caregivers' wishes and
            expectations and can obey simple requests and commands. p. 200

Chapter 7: Answers

7.1   B   During early and middle childhood, X-rays of epiphyses, or growth centers in which cartilage hardens into bone, permit doctors to estimate children's skeletal age, or progress toward physical maturity. pp. 208-209

7.2   B   Twins are more likely than ordinary siblings to differ in handedness. The hand preference of each twin is related to body position during the prenatal period. pp. 210-211

7.3   D   Infants born with a deficiency of thyroxine must receive it at once or they will be mentally retarded. At later ages, children with too little thyroxine grow at a below-average rate. By then, the central nervous system is no longer affected, since the most rapid period of brain development is complete. p. 212

7.4   B   Illness affects physical growth because it limits the body's ability to absorb foods. p. 215

7.5   D   Although injury deaths have steadily declined in nearly all developed countries during the past 30 years, they have dropped only slightly in the United States. p. 217

7.6   D   From an early age, boys and girls are usually encouraged into different physical activities. For example, fathers often play catch with their sons but seldom do so with their daughters. Baseballs and footballs are purchased for boys; jump ropes, hula hoops, and skates for girls. p. 220

7.7   D   In early pretending, toddlers use only realistic objects. Around age 2, they use less realistic toys more frequently. Sometime during the third year, children can imagine objects and events without support from the real world. p. 222

7.8   B   Preoperational children fail the conservation of liquid task because they center on the height of the water, failing to realize that all changes in height are compensated by changes in width. pp. 223-224

7.9   B   Recent studies indicate that Piaget overestimated children's animistic beliefs because he asked children about objects with which they have little direct experience, such as the clouds and sun. Children as young as 3 rarely think that very familiar inanimate objects, such as rocks and crayons, are alive. p. 225

7.10   C   In a Piagetian classroom, children are encouraged to discover for themselves
through spontaneous interaction with the environment. A Piagetian
classroom does not try to speed up development. Instead Piaget believed that
appropriate learning experiences build on children's current thinking. p. 227

7.11   D   Vygotsky believed that preschoolers speak to themselves for self-guidance
and self-direction. p. 228

7.12   C   According to Vygotsky, in make-believe play, children learn to follow
internal ideas and social rules rather than their immediate impulses. For
example, a child pretending to go to sleep follows the rules of bedtime
behavior. p. 229

7.13   A   Cross-cultural research shows that verbal communication may not be the
most important means, in some cultures, through which thinking develops.
For example, children learning to sail a canoe in Micronesia or weave a
garment on a foot loom in Guatemala gain more from direct observation than
from joint participation with and verbal guidance by adults. pp. 229-230

7.14   A   Scripts do not facilitate children's recall of specific instances of repeated
experiences because they refer to general rather than specific representations
of familiar, repeated events. p. 231

7.15   B   Children with infantile autism, who are indifferent to other people and
display poor knowledge of social rules, seem to be impaired in mental
understanding. pp. 232-233

7.16   C   Cross-cultural research suggests that basic counting knowledge emerges
universally around the world. However, children acquire it at different rates,
depending on the availability of informal experiences in their everyday lives.
p. 234

7.17   A   Research shows that young children in child-centered preschools score better
on assessments of language, academic, motor, and social skills than children
in academic preschools. p. 236

7.18   C   Research on Head Start has shown that mental test scores and achievement
begin to decline during the first 2 to 3 years of elementary school.
Nonetheless, children who have received intervention remain ahead on
measures of real-life school adjustment into adolescence. p. 237

7.19   C   According to the principle of mutual exclusivity, when children hear an
unfamiliar word, they are most likely to attach the new word to an unknown
object. This is because they assume that words refer to entirely separate and
nonoverlapping categories. p. 239

7.20   C   Expansions are adult responses that elaborate on a child's utterance,
           increasing its complexity. Recasts are adult responses that restructure a
           child's incorrect speech into an appropriate form. p. 241

Chapter 8: Answers

8.1   A   According to Erikson, the negative outcome of early childhood is an overly strict superego, one that causes children to feel too much guilt because they have been threatened, criticized, and punished excessively by adults. p. 249

8.2   A   Two distinct aspects of the self that emerge during the preschool years are the I-self, which is children's own subjective experience of being, and the me-self, which is knowledge and evaluation of the self's characteristics. p. 249

8.3   D   Preschoolers tend to rate their own self-esteem as extremely high and underestimate the difficult of tasks. High self-esteem contributes greatly to preschoolers' initiative during a period in which they must master many new skills. p. 250

8.4   C   Both children are likely to feel guilty because preschoolers are likely to feel guilty for any act that can be described as wrongdoing, even if it was accidental. p. 252

8.5   A   Although nonsocial activity declines with age, it is still the most frequent form of behavior among 3- to 4-year olds. Even among kindergartners it continues to take up as much as a third of children's free-play time. p. 254

8.6   C   Young children explore and gain control over fear-arousing experiences when they play doctor or dentist or pretend to search for monsters in a magical forest. As a result, they are better able to understand the feelings of others and regulate their own. p. 254

8.7   B   Preschoolers regard friendship as pleasurable play and sharing of toys. Friendship does not yet have a long-term enduring quality based on mutual trust. p. 255

8.8   B   Parents who phrase their directives positively and politely tend to have preschoolers who are successful in influencing their peers. p. 255

8.9   D   In Freud's psychoanalytic theory, children form a superego, or conscience, by identifying with the same-sex parent and internalizing his or her moral standards. p. 256

8.10   B   Children admire and therefore tend to select competent, powerful models to imitate—the reason they are especially willing to copy the behavior of older peers and adults. p. 258

8.11 D   In contrast to the psychoanalytic and behaviorist approaches to morality that focus on how children acquire ready-made standards of good conduct from adults, the cognitive-developmental perspective regards children as active thinkers about social rules. p. 260

8.12 C   Relational aggression is aggression that damages another person's peer relationships, as in social exclusion and rumor spreading. p. 260

8.13 B   Preschool and school-age girls are not less aggressive than boys. Instead, they are likely to express their hostility differently—through relational aggression. p. 261

8.14 A   Longitudinal research reveals that highly aggressive children have a greater appetite for violent TV. As they watch more, they become increasingly likely to resort to hostile ways of solving problems. pp. 261-262

8.15 A   Mothers more often label emotions when talking to girls, thereby teaching them to "tune in" to others' feelings. In contrast, they more often explain emotions, noting causes and consequences, to boy—an approach that emphasizes why it is important to control the expression of emotion. p. 265

8.16 D   During the preschool years, boys who frequently engage in "gender-inappropriate" activities—for example, playing with dolls—are likely to be ignored by other boys even when they engage in "masculine" activities. p. 265

8.17 A   Masculine and androgynous children have high self-esteem, whereas feminine children often think poorly of themselves, perhaps because many feminine traits are not highly valued in our society. pp. 265-266

8.18 A   Because Athena's schemas lead her to conclude that "cars and trucks are not for me," she responds by avoiding "gender-inappropriate" toys. p. 266

8.19 D   In several studies, physical discipline in early childhood predicted aggression during the school years only for Caucasian-American children. These results suggest ethnic differences in how children view parental behavior that can modify its consequences. For example, African-American parents who use firm discipline often combine it with warmth, which predicts favorable adjustment. p. 270

8.20 B   Parents Anonymous combats child maltreatment by providing social supports. Its local chapters offer self-help group meetings, daily phone calls, and regular home visits to relieve social isolation and teach alternative child-rearing skills. p. 272

Chapter 9: Answers

9.1   D   During middle childhood, the lower portion of the body is growing fastest. p. 280

9.2   A   Next to already existing obesity, time spent watching television is the best predictor of future obesity among school-age children. Television greatly reduces the time devoted to physical exercise, and TV ads encourage children to eat fattening, unhealthy snacks. p. 284

9.3   A   Motor vehicle accidents are the leading cause of injury in middle childhood, whereas bicycle accidents are the second leading cause. pp. 285-286

9.4   B   In middle childhood, girls outperform boys on skills that depend on agility and balance, such as jumping and hopping. Boys outperform girls on all other gross motor skills. p. 288

9.5   D   Because competitive sports are unlikely to reach the least physically fit youngsters, research suggests that physical education programs should emphasize informal games that most children can perform well. p. 289

9.6   B   Piaget regarded conservation as the single most important achievement of the concrete operational stage because it provides clear evidence of operations—mental actions that obey logical rules. p. 291

9.7   D   Cross-cultural research indicates that specific cultural and school practices have a great deal to do with the mastery of Piagetian tasks. p. 292

9.8   B   Cognitive inhibition—the ability to resist interference from irrelevant information—supports many information processing skills by clearing unnecessary information from working memory. p. 293

9.9   C   This is an example of elaboration. This memory strategy involves creating a relationship between two or more pieces of information that are not members of the same category. pp. 295-296

9.10   A   Cross-cultural research indicates that people in non-Western cultures who have no formal schooling do not use or benefit from instruction in memory strategies. p. 296

9.11   C   Cognitive self-regulation refers to the process of monitoring progress toward a goal, checking outcomes, and redirecting unsuccessful efforts. p. 297

9.12   A   Teachers who advocate a whole-language approach argue that from the
           beginning, children should be exposed to text in its complete form—stories,
           poems, letters, posters, and lists—so they can appreciate the communicative
           function of written language. pp. 297-298

9.13   C   Cross-cultural research with Asian children suggests that American math
           instruction may have gone too far in emphasizing computational drill and in
           de-emphasizing underlying math concepts. p. 298

9.14   D   Factor analysis is a statistical procedure used for studying the underlying
           mental abilities associated with intelligence tests. p. 299

9.15   C   Attempts to change intelligence tests by eliminating fact-oriented verbal
           tasks and relying only on spatial reasoning and performance items (believed
           to be less culturally loaded) have not raised the IQ score of low-SES
           minority children very much. p. 303

9.16   C   Bilingual children do better than others on tests of selective attention,
           analytic reasoning, concept formation, and cognitive flexibility. p. 305

9.17   D   Compared to children in traditional classrooms, those in open classrooms
           show greater gains in critical thinking. p. 307

9.18   A   When teachers hold inaccurate views, low achievers are more affected than
           high achievers. High-achieving pupils can fall back on their history of
           success when a teacher is critical. p. 308-309

9.19   B   The Individuals with Disabilities Education Act mandates that schools place
           children with learning disabilities in the least restrictive environments that
           meet their educational needs. The law led to a rapid increase in
           mainstreaming of pupils with learning disabilities in regular classrooms for
           part of the school day. p. 309

9.20   A   Cross-cultural research shows that as they move up through the grades in
           school, American children drop in mathematics and science achievement
           relative to children in other countries such as Hong Kong, Japan, Korea, and
           Taiwan. p. 312

Chapter 10: Answers

10.1   D   According to Erikson, the danger during middle childhood is inferiority. This sense of inadequacy can develop when experiences with teachers and peers are so negative that they destroy their feelings of competency and mastery. p. 320

10.2   C   Preschoolers have very high self-esteem. As children move into middle childhood, their self-esteem adjusts to a more realistic level as the result of much more feedback about their performance in different activities compared with that of their peers. p. 322

10.3   C   Children who make mastery-oriented attributions believe their successes are due to ability and they attribute failure to factors that can be changed, such as insufficient effort. p. 323

10.4   C   During middle childhood, children do not report guilt for any mishap, as they did at younger ages, but only for intentional wrongdoings. p. 325

10.5   B   According to Damon, children's reasoning about distributive justice follows an age-related, three-step sequence: equality (5 to 6 years); merit (6 to 7 years); and benevolence (8 years). p. 326

10.6   C   When children challenge parental authority, they typically do so within the personal domain. p. 327

10.7   B   Peer groups generate unique values and standards for behavior and create a social structure of leaders and followers that ensure group goals will be met. p. 327

10.8   D   Preschoolers tend to report they have lots of friends, whereas by age 8 or 9, children have only a handful of people they call friends. p. 328

10.9   B   Rejected-aggressive children are deficient in social understanding. For example, they tend to misinterpret the innocent behavior of peers as hostile, blame others for their social difficulties, and act on their angry feelings. p. 329

10.10   D   Controversial children are hostile and disruptive. Even though they are disliked by a large number of peers, they have qualities that protect them from social exclusion. As a result, they are happy and comfortable with peer relationships. p. 331

10.11   D   Both children and adults are fairly tolerant of girls' violations of gender
            roles. However, they judge boys' violations (e.g., playing house) as just as
            bad as violating a moral rule. p. 331

10.12   C   Nyansongo children of both sexes perform "feminine" activities. Their
            greater freedom and independence lead girls to score higher than girls of
            other village and tribal cultures in dominance, assertiveness, and playful
            roughhousing. Boys' caregiving responsibilities mean that they frequently
            engage in help giving and emotional support. p. 332

10.13   C   A critical ingredient of coregulation is that parents must strengthen in their
            children the abilities that will allow them to avoid undue risks and know
            when they need parental support and guidance. p. 333

10.14   A   When siblings are close in age and the same sex, parental comparisons are
            more frequent, resulting in more quarreling and antagonism. p. 333

10.15   D   Compared with agemates who have siblings, only children do better in
            school and attain higher levels of education. One reason may be that only
            children have somewhat closer relationships with parents, who exert more
            pressure for mastery and accomplishment. p. 334

10.16   A   Because boys are more active and noncompliant—behaviors that increase
            with exposure to parental conflict and inconsistent discipline—boys in
            mother-custody families are most likely to experience serious adjustment
            problems. p. 336

10.17   A   The overriding factor in positive adjustment following divorce is effective
            parenting—in particular, how well the custodial parent handles stress,
            shields the child from conflict, and uses authoritative parenting. p. 336

10.18   D   Maternal employment does not reduce the time school-age children spend
            with their mothers and it results in more time with fathers. More parental
            contact is associated with higher achievement, mature social behavior, and
            a more flexible view of gender roles. p. 338

10.19   D   Typically, children who develop school phobia tend to be middle-class and
            have average or above achievement. They feel severe apprehension about
            attending school, often accompanied by physical complaints that disappear
            once they are allowed to remain home. p. 339

10.20   C   Research on child sexual abuse indicates that the abuser is most often a
            parent or someone the parent knows well. Often he is a father, stepfather,
            or live-in boyfriend. p. 341

Chapter 11: Answers

11.1   A   Freud called adolescence the *genital stage*, a period in which instinctual drives reawaken and shift to the genital region of the body, resulting in psychological conflict and volatile, unpredictable behavior. p. 350

11.2   B   By midadolescence, for example, very few girls perform as well as the average boy in such skills as running speed, broad jump, and throwing distance. And practically no boys score as low as the average girl. p. 353

11.3   B   In females, a sharp rise in body weight and fat may trigger sexual maturation. Girls who begin serious athletic training at young ages or who eat very little (both of which reduce the percentage of body fat) often show greatly delayed menstruation. In contrast, overweight girls typically start menstruating earlier. p. 355

11.4   A   Furthermore, compared with the moods of adults, adolescents' feelings were less stable. But teenagers also moved from one situation to another more often, and their mood swings were strongly related to these changes. Taken together, these findings suggest that situational factors may combine with hormonal influences to affect teenagers' moodiness. p. 356

11.5   B   In one study, early maturing sixth-grade girls felt better about themselves when they attended kindergarten through sixth grade schools (K-6) rather than kindergarten through eighth grade (K-8) schools, where they could mix with older adolescents. A New Zealand study found that delinquency among early maturing girls was greatly reduced in all-girl schools, which limit opportunities to associate with norm-violating peers (most of whom are older boys). p. 358

11.6   C   The most common nutritional problem of adolescence is iron deficiency. p. 359

11.7   B   Anorexics have an extremely distorted body image. Even after they have become severely underweight, they conclude that they are fat. p. 359

11.8   C   Early and frequent teenage sexual activity is linked to a wide range of personal, family, peer, and educational characteristics. These include early physical maturation, parental divorce, large family size, sexually active friends and older siblings, poor school performance, lower educational aspirations, and tendency to engage in norm-violating acts, including alcohol and drug use and delinquency. p. 361

11.9   B   Male homosexuality tends to be more common on the maternal than
            paternal side of families. This suggests that it might be X-linked. Indeed,
            one gene-mapping study found that among 40 pairs of homosexual brothers,
            33 (88 percent) had an identical segment of DNA on the X chromosome.
            One or several genes in that region might predispose males to become
            homosexual. p. 363

11.10 A   Only 50 percent of adolescent mothers graduate with either a diploma or
            general equivalency degree. When teenage mothers do marry, they are
            more likely to divorce than are their peers who delay child bearing. Often
            they have additional out-of-wedlock births in quick succession. Because
            many pregnant girls do not receive early prenatal care, their babies often
            experience prenatal and birth complications, especially low birth weight. p.
            366

11.11 B   Teenagers in greatest danger of STD are the same ones who tend to engage
            in irresponsible sexual behavior—poverty-stricken young people who feel a
            sense of hopelessness about their lives. p. 364-365

11.12 D   By early adolescence, peer encouragement—friends who use and provide
            access to illegal substances—is a strong predictor of substance abuse. p. -
            369

11.13 D   Concrete operational children experiment unsystematically. p. 371

11.14 C   They (young children) fail to grasp the *logical necessity* of propositional
            reasoning—that the validity of conclusions drawn from premises rests on
            the rules of logic, not on real-world confirmation. p. 372

11.15 D   Research reveals that adolescents develop formal operational thinking in a
            similar, step-by-step fashion on different tasks. Adolescents mastered
            component skills in sequential order by expanding their metacognitive
            awareness. Over time, adolescents combined separate skills into a smoothly
            functioning system. Scientific reasoning develops gradually out of many
            specific experiences. But even at advanced levels of education, scientific
            reasoning is rarely taught directly. p. 373

11.16 A   As teenagers imagine what others must be thinking, two distorted images of
            the relation between self and other appear. The first is called the imaginary
            audience. Young teenagers regard themselves as always onstage. They are
            convinced that they are the focus of everyone else's attention and concern.
            As a result, they become extremely self-conscious, often going to great
            lengths to avoid embarrassment. p. 375

11.17   B   Although heredity is involved, social pressures contribute to girls'
            underrepresentation among the mathematically talented. Long before sex
            differences in math achievement appear, both boys and girls view math as a
            "masculine" subject. p. 376

11.18   C   Adolescents who must cope with added life stresses, such as family
            disruptions or a shift in residence, around the time they change schools are
            at greatest risk for academic and emotional difficulties. p. 378

11.19   C   A case study of six inner-city, poverty-stricken African-American
            adolescents who were high-achieving and optimistic about their futures
            revealed that they were intensely aware of oppression but believed in
            striving to alter their social position. Parents, relatives, and teachers had
            convinced them through discussion and example that injustice should not be
            tolerated and that together, blacks could overcome it—a perspective that
            facilitated academic motivation in the face of peer pressures against doing
            well in school. p. 381

11.20   B   *Participation in extracurricular activities.* Another way of helping
            marginal students is to draw them into the community life of the school.
            Potential dropouts are far more likely to participate, feel needed, gain
            recognition for their abilities, and remain until graduation. p. 383

Chapter 12: Answers

12.1   A   Current theorists agree that the adolescent's questioning of the self's values, plans, and priorities is necessary for a mature identity, but they no longer refer to this process as a "crisis." "Exploration" better describes the typical adolescent's gradual, uneventful approach to identity formation. p. 390

12.2   C   Those who lack a sense of industry fail to select a vocation that matches their interests and skills. p. 390

12.3   A   By middle to late adolescence, the capacity for abstract thinking permits teenagers to combine their various traits into an organized system. And they begin to use qualifiers ("I have a fairly quick temper," "I'm not thoroughly honest"), revealing their awareness that psychological qualities often change from one situation to the next. p. 391

12.4   B   Identity-diffused individuals lack clear direction. They are not committed to values and goals, nor are they actively trying to reach them. p. 392

12.5   C   Classrooms that promote high-level thinking; extracurricular and community activities that enable teenagers to take on responsible roles; teachers and counselors who encourage low-SES students to go to college; and vocational training programs that immerse young people in the real world of adult work foster identity achievement. p. 393

12.6   A   Children who have made the transition to autonomous morality realize that people can have different perspectives on moral matters and that intentions, not just outcomes, should serve as the basis for judging behavior. p. 396

12.7   C   Individuals at the postconventional level, which includes Stage 5 (the social contract orientation), move beyond unquestioning support for the laws and rules of their own society. At Stage 5, individuals regard laws and rules as flexible instruments for furthering human purposes. p. 398

12.8   D   The highest level of moral reasoning is still a matter of speculation and may represent a reflective, philosophical orientation that lies beyond the realm of commonplace, spontaneous moral thought. p. 398

12.9   A   In one investigation, adolescents and adults in India showed the same pattern of movement through Kohlberg's stages as their American agemates, and just as many or more reached the postconventional level. Still, the East Indian participants often dealt with moral conflicts in ways that did not fit neatly into Kohlberg's scheme. Kohlberg's theory does not capture all aspects of moral thinking in every culture. p. 400

12.10   B   On hypothetical dilemmas as well as everyday moral problems, themes of justice and caring appear in the responses of both sexes. p. 399

12.11   C   Overall, androgynous adolescents tend to be psychologically healthier. p. 401

12.12   B   Adolescents are not the only family members undergoing a major life transition. Many parents are in their forties and are reassessing their own lives. p. 402

12.13   C   Teenagers stress two characteristics of friendship. The first, and most important, is intimacy. Second, more than younger children, teenagers want their friends to be loyal. p. 403

12.14   A   Cultural variations in group norms also exist. These findings indicate that many peer group values are extensions of ones acquired at home. p. 405

12.15   C   Homosexual youths face special challenges in initiating and maintaining visible romances. Their first dating relationships seem to be short-lived and to involve little emotional commitment for different reasons than those of heterosexuals: They fear peer harassment and rejection. p. 406

12.16   A   In one study of nearly 400 junior and senior high school students, adolescents felt greatest pressure to conform to the most obvious aspects of the peer culture—dressing and grooming like everyone else and participating in social activities. p. 406

12.17   A   Early maturing girls, who often have a negative body image and are less well liked by peers, are prone to depression, especially when they face other life stresses. p. 408

12.18   A   Belief in the personal fable leads many depressed young people to conclude that no one could possibly understand the intense pain they feel. As a result, their despair, hopelessness, and isolation deepen. p. 409

12.19   A   One of the most consistent findings about delinquent youths is that their family environments are low in warmth, high in conflict, and characterized by inconsistent discipline. Beginning in early childhood, these forms of child rearing breed antisocial behavior. p. 412

12.20   B   Treatment models that work best are lengthy and intensive and use problem-focused methods that teach cognitive and social skills needed to overcome family, peer, and school difficulties. p. 412

Chapter 13: Answers

13.1   C   Once body structures reach maximum capacity and efficiency in the teens and twenties, biological aging, or senescence, begins—genetically influenced declines in the functioning of organs and systems that are universal in all members of our species. p. 420

13.2   D   Sociability—expected to foster longevity—did just the opposite! Cheerful, "happy-go-lucky" children grew into adults more likely to smoke, drink, and take risks—behaviors known to shorten length of life. p. 423

13.3   B   According to current estimates, maximum lifespan varies between 70 and 110 years for most people, with 85 or 90 about average. p. 422

13.4   B   When researchers estimate active lifespan, they find that Americans can expect an average of 64 years of vigorous, healthy life. p. 423

13.5   C   The strongest evidence for this view comes from research showing that human cells allowed to divide in the laboratory have a lifespan of 50 divisions plus or minus 10. With each duplication, the cells lose more of a special type of DNA—called *telomeres,* located at the ends of chromosomes—that is vital for cell duplication, until the cells no longer duplicate at all. p. 424

13.6   D   If atherosclerosis is present, it usually begins early in life, progresses during middle adulthood, and culminates in serious illness. p. 425

13.7   A   As longitudinal research with several hundred thousand participants reveals, young and middle-aged adults at low risk for heart disease, defined by not smoking, low blood cholesterol, and normal blood pressure, show 40 to 60 percent reduced death rates over the next 16 to 22 years. p. 425

13.8   C   Athletic tasks that require speed of limb movement, explosive strength, and gross body coordination—sprinting, jumping, and tennis—peak in the early twenties. Those that depend on endurance, arm–hand steadiness, and aiming—long-distance running, baseball, and golf—peak in the late twenties and early thirties. p. 427

13.9   D   Fat adults suffer enormous social discrimination. They are less likely to find mates and be rented apartments, given financial aid for college, and offered jobs. p. 430

13.10   C   Besides reducing body fat and building muscle, exercise fosters resistance to disease. Frequent bouts of moderate-intensity exercise enhance the immune response. p. 432

13.11   C   In men, alcoholism usually begins in the teens and early twenties and
worsens over the following decade. In women, its onset is typically later, in
the twenties and thirties, and its course more variable. p. 433

13.12   D   As number of sex partners increases, satisfaction declines sharply. These
findings challenge the stereotype of marriage as sexually dull and people
with many partners as having the "hottest" sex. p. 435

13.13   B   In a national sample of over 6,000 American college students, 44 percent of
women reported having experienced sexual coercion and 19 percent of men
said they had obtained sex through force. p. 437

13.14   D   Helping people who are isolated develop and maintain satisfying social ties
has many stress-buffering effects. p. 439

13.15   C   Older students were aware of a diversity of opinions on almost any topic.
They moved toward relativistic thinking, viewing all knowledge as
embedded in a framework of thought. As a result, they gave up the
possibility of absolute truth in favor of multiple truths, each relative to its
context. p. 440

13.16   A   The course of creativity varies across disciplines. For example, artists and
musicians typically show an early rise in creativity, perhaps because they do
not need to undergo extensive formal education before they begin to
produce. Academic scholars and scientists usually display their
achievements later and over a longer time, since they must earn a higher
degree and spend years doing research to make worthwhile contributions.
pp. 442

13.17   C   Findings on five mental abilities showed the typical cross-sectional drop
after the mid-thirties. p. 443

13.18   B   Residential living is one of the most consistent determinants of change
because it maximizes involvement in the educational and social systems of
the institution. p. 444

13.19   C   Dominic is in the realistic period (late adolescence and early adulthood). By
the early twenties, the economic and practical realities of adulthood are just
around the corner, and young people start to narrow their options. At first,
many do so through further *exploration,* gathering more information about a
set of possibilities that blends with their personal characteristics. Then they
enter a final phase of *crystallization* in which they focus on a general
vocational category. Within it, they experiment for a period of time before
settling on a single occupation. pp. 445

13.20   D   Unlike Western European nations, the United States has no widespread
            training system to prepare its youths for skilled business and industrial
            occupations and manual trades. Inspired by successful programs in Western
            Europe, youth apprenticeship strategies that coordinate on-the-job training
            with classroom instruction are being considered as an important dimension
            of educational reform in the United States. Bringing together the worlds of
            schooling and work offers many benefits. These include helping non-
            college-bound young people establish productive lives right after
            graduation. p. 448

Chapter 14: Answers

14.1   A   Without a sense of independence, people define themselves only in terms of their partner and sacrifice self-respect and initiative. p. 456

14.2   D   The primary task of a structure-building period is to select and integrate components in ways that enhance one's life. p. 458

14.3   B   Levinson describes age 33 to 40 as a period of settling down. To create the culminating life structure of early adulthood, men emphasize certain relationships and aspirations and make others secondary or set them aside. In doing so, they try to establish a stable niche in society by anchoring themselves more firmly in family, occupation, and community. At the same time, they advance within the structure. "Settling down" however, does not accurately describe women's experiences during their thirties. Many remain highly unsettled because of the addition of an occupational or relationship commitment that must be integrated into their life structure. Not until middle adulthood do many women attain the stability typical of men in their thirties. p. 459

14.4   D   According to Vaillant, men in their fifties became "keepers of meaning," or guardians of their culture. p. 459

14.5   C   Following a social clock of some kind seems to foster confidence during early adulthood because it guarantees that the young person will engage in the work of society, develop skills, and increase in understanding of the self and others. p. 460

14.6   A   Commitment is the cognitive component of love. It leads partners to decide that they are in love and to maintain that love. p. 461

14.7   B   An important feature of the communication in higher-quality relationships is constructive conflict resolution—raising issues gently and avoiding the escalation of negative interaction sparked by criticism, contempt, defensiveness, and stonewalling. These negative escalation cycles are one of the strongest predictors of marital distress and future divorce. p. 462

14.8   D   Men report barriers to intimacy with other men. For example, they indicate that they sometimes feel in competition with male friends and are therefore unwilling to disclose any weaknesses. p. 464

14.9   C   As young people marry and need to invest less time in developing a romantic partnership, siblings become more frequent companions than they were in adolescence. Often there is a spillover between friend and sibling roles. p. 465

14.10   C   Separated, divorced, or widowed adults are lonelier than their married,
            cohabiting, or single counterparts, suggesting that loneliness is especially
            intense after loss of an intimate tie. p. 465

14.11   A   Nearly half of young adults return home for a brief time after initial leaving.
            Those who departed to marry are least likely to return. p. 466\

14.12   A   Entry of children into the family usually causes the roles of husband and
            wife to become more traditional. p. 472

14.13   D   In a longitudinal study of over 2,000 couples diverse in age, SES, and
            ethnicity, marital quality was the strongest predictor of parenting
            satisfaction. p. 473

14.14   B   Americans are more open to cohabitation than they were in the past,
            although attitudes are not yet as positive as they are in Western Europe.
            Largely as a result of cultural ambivalence about cohabitation, American
            cohabitors differ from people who are married or living in separate
            residences. They are less religious, more politically liberal, more
            androgynous, and have had more sexual partners. Overall, they are more
            likely to endorse and engage in nonconventional behavior. p. 476

14.15   A   Voluntarily childless adults are just as content with their lives as are parents
            who have rewarding relationships with their children. Childlessness
            interferes with adjustment and life satisfaction only when it is beyond a
            person's control. p. 477

14.16   C   Finding a new partner contributes most to the life satisfaction of divorced
            adults. But it is more crucial for men, who show more positive adjustment
            in the context of marriage than on their own. p. 478

14.17   B   Stepfathers with children of their own have an easier time than stepmothers.
            They establish positive ties with stepchildren relatively quickly, perhaps
            because they feel less pressure to plunge into parenting than do stepmothers.
            At the same time, they have had enough experience to know how to build a
            warm parent-child relationship. p. 479

14.18   A   When children were adopted or conceived through reproductive
            technologies, partners tend to be more involved than when children resulted
            from a previous heterosexual relationship. p. 480

14.19   C   As new workers become aware of the gap between their expectations and
            reality, resignations are common. p. 481

14.20   D   At age 60, women among the highly gifted "Termites" who reported the
            highest levels of life satisfaction had developed rewarding careers. p. 482

Chapter 15: Answers

15.1   B   Men's hearing declines earlier and at a faster rate than women's, a difference thought to be due to exposure to environmental noise in male-dominated occupations. p. 494

15.2   D   Our skin consists of three layers: the epidermis, the dermis, and the hypodermis, which is an inner fatty layer that adds to the soft lines and shape of the skin. p. 494

15.3   B   Advantages of hormone replacement therapy are clear: protection against bone deterioration and cardiovascular disease and a reduction in certain discomforts of the climacteric, such as mood fluctuations and hot flashes. HRT may also improve memory and other aspects of cognition in postmenopausal women. And it may help maintain cognitive functioning in late adulthood. p. 495

15.4   D   Testosterone production, along with its effects on male sex organs and sexual interest, remains stable throughout adulthood in healthy men who continue to engage in sexual activity (which stimulates cells that release testosterone). p. 496

15.5   C   The sexual activity—well-being association is probably bidirectional. Sex is more likely to occur in the context of a good marriage, and couples having sex often probably view their relationship more positively. p. 496

15.6   C   Although the incidence of many types of cancer is currently leveling off or declining, cancer mortality was on the rise for many decades, largely because of a dramatic increase in lung cancer due to cigarette smoking. p. 498

15.7   D   In some individuals, indigestionlike or crushing chest pains, called angina pectoris, reveal an oxygen-deprived heart. p. 500

15.8   D   Recent findings suggest that expressed hostility—frequent angry outbursts; rude, disagreeable behavior; and critical and condescending nonverbal cues during social interaction—leads to greater cardiovascular arousal, health complaints, and illness. p. 502

15.9   C   In problem-centered coping, people appraise the situation as changeable, identify the difficulty, and decide what to do about it. p. 503

15.10   D   Researchers have studied a set of three personal qualities—control, commitment, and challenge—that, together, they call hardiness. p. 504

15.11   B   Researchers believe that the ideal of a sexually attractive woman—smooth skin, good muscle tone, and lustrous hair—is at the heart of the double standard of aging. p. 505

15.12   C   Crystallized intelligence refers to skills that depend on accumulated knowledge and experience, good judgment, and mastery of social conventions. On intelligence tests, vocabulary, general information, verbal analogy, and logical reasoning items measure crystallized intelligence. p. 507

15.13   A   There are several reasons why longitudinal research reveals stability in a variety of crystallized and fluid abilities during middle adulthood despite declines in basic information-processing skills. One of the reasons listed in the text is that adults often find ways to compensate for cognitive weaknesses by drawing on their cognitive strengths. p. 508

15.14   A   According to the neural network view, as neurons in the brain die, breaks in neural networks occur. The brain adapts by forming bypasses—new synaptic connections that go around the breaks but are less efficient. p. 509

15.15   D   Whether given lists of words or digits or meaningful prose passages to learn, middle-aged and older adults recall less than young adults, although memory for prose suffers less than memory for list items. p. 510

15.16   D   Expertise is not just the province of the highly educated and those who rise to the top of administrative ladders. It can emerge in any field of endeavor. p. 511

15.17   B   Research on everyday problem solving reveals that it peaks between 40 and 59 years of age and may be sustained even longer. p. 511

15.18   B   Research on everyday problem solving reveals that middle-aged and older adults select better strategies than do young adults. From middle age on adults place greater emphasis on thinking through a practical problem—trying to understand it better, to solve it through logical analysis, to reinterpret it from a different perspective. p. 512

15.19   A   Research shows that the impact of a challenging job on cognitive growth is not greater for young adults. People in their fifties and early sixties gain as much as do those in their twenties and thirties. p. 514

15.20   A   Social supports for returning students can make the difference between continuing in school and dropping out. p. 515

Chapter 16: Answers

16.1   B   The generative adult combines his or her need for self-expression with a need for communion, integrating personal goals with the welfare of the larger social environment. p. 522

16.2   A   People with a sense of stagnation are unable to contribute to society's welfare because they place their own comfort and security above challenge and sacrifice. Their self-absorption is expressed in many ways—through lack of involvement with and concern for young people (including their own children); through a focus on what they can get from others rather than what they can give; and through little interest in being productive at work, developing their talents, or bettering the world in other ways. p. 523

16.3   D   Especially for women, the gap between subjective and objective age widens over time. p. 526

16.4   C   When poverty, unemployment, and lack of a respected place in society dominate the life course, energies are directed toward survival rather than pursuit of a satisfying life structure. Even adults whose jobs are secure and who live in pleasant neighborhoods may find that employment conditions place too much emphasis on productivity and profit and too little on the meaning of work, thereby restricting possibilities for growth. p. 526

16.5   D   Research suggests wide individual differences in response to midlife, but sharp disruption and agitation are more the exception than the rule. p. 527

16.6   D   The few adults who are in crisis typically have had early adulthoods in which gender roles, family pressures, or low-income and poverty severely limited their ability to attain reasonable satisfaction of personal needs and goals, either at home or in the wider world. p. 528

16.7   C   The mid-life transition is simply an adaptation to life events—external pressures that affect many people during the middle years, such as children growing up, reaching the crest of a career, and impending retirement. p. 528

16.8   B   Life events are no longer as age graded as they were in the past. Timing varies enough that they cannot be the single cause of midlife change. p. 528

16.9   D   Most middle-aged people no longer desire to be the best and the most successful. Instead, they are largely concerned with performance of roles and responsibilities already begun—being "competent at work," "a good husband and father," "able to put my children through the colleges of their choice," and not being "in poor health" or "without enough money to meet my daily needs." p. 529

16.10   C   In this study, three traits—self-acceptance, autonomy, and environmental mastery—increased from early to middle adulthood. p. 529

16.11   A   Middle-aged individuals are more likely to look for the "silver lining" or positive side of a difficult situation, to postpone action to permit evaluation of alternative courses of action, to anticipate and plan ways to handle future discomforts, and to use humor to express ideas and feelings without negative effects on others. p.529-530

16.12   C   Individuals who are high on the trait of agreeableness are soft-hearted, trusting, generous, acquiescent, lenient, and good-natured. p. 533

16.13   A   Partly because Americans between 45 and 54 have the highest average annual income, and partly because the time between departure of the last child and retirement is so long, the contemporary social view of marriage in midlife has become one of expansion and new horizons. p. 534

16.14   A   Parents who have developed gratifying alternative activities typically welcome their children's adult status. A strong work orientation, especially, predicts gains in life satisfaction after children depart from the home. p. 535

16.15   D   They are called the sandwich generation because they are "sandwiched," or squeezed, between the needs of aging parents and financially dependent children. p. 540

16.16   D   Parental illness can have a profound impact on sibling closeness. p. 542

16.17   C   Very young adults (18- to 24-year-olds) are more likely than other age groups to view government programs serving the elderly as too costly. But having had frequent contact with grandparents increases their endorsement of these benefits. p. 543

16.18   A   Intrinsic satisfaction—contentment with the work itself—shows a strong age-related gain. Extrinsic satisfaction—for example, with supervision, pay, and promotions—changes very little. p. 544

16.19   B   Social support is vital for reducing stress and reassuring middle-aged job seekers of their worth. p. 547

16.20   C   Retirement leads to a loss of two important work-related rewards—income and status—and to a change in many other aspects of life. Like other life transitions, retirement is often stressful. p. 547

Chapter 17: Answers

17.1   D   Chronological age is an imperfect indicator of functional age, or actual competence and performance. Because people age biologically at different rates, experts distinguish between the young-old elderly, who appear physically young for their advanced years, and the old-old elderly, who show signs of decline. p. 556

17.2   C   The difference is largely due to high birthrates among America's poverty-stricken groups and less effective public policies ensuring health and well-being throughout the lifespan. p. 557

17.3   C   Several large-scale studies suggest that a diet rich in green, leafy vegetables reduces the risk of macular degeneration and slows vision loss in those with the condition. p. 560

17.4   A   Although hearing loss has less impact on self-care than does vision, it affects safety and enjoyment of life. The decline in speech perception has the greatest impact on life satisfaction. p. 562

17.5   B   With age, lung tissue loses its elasticity. The lungs fill and empty less efficiently, causing the blood to absorb less oxygen and give off less carbon dioxide. p. 563

17.6   D   Until age 70 or 80, men experience more sleep disturbances than do women for several reasons. First, enlargement of the prostate gland, which occurs in almost all aging men, constricts the ureters and leads to a need to urinate more often, including during the night. Second, men are more prone to sleep apnea, a condition in which breathing ceases for 10 seconds or longer, resulting in many brief awakenings. The incidence of sleep apnea in elderly men is high. Finally, periodic rapid movement of the legs sometimes accompanies sleep apnea but also occurs at other times of night. Called "restless legs," these movements may be due to muscle tension, reduced circulation, or age-related changes in motor areas of the brain. p. 564

17.7   C   Weight generally drops after age 60 due to additional loss in lean body mass (bone density and muscle), which is heavier than the fat deposits accumulating on the torso. p. 564-565

17.8   B   Longitudinal research reveals that disability need not follow a path toward further disability and dependency. In several studies, 12 to 20 percent of elders with disabilities showed improvement 2 to 6 years later. p. 566

17.9   D   The physical changes of late life lead to an increased need for certain
               nutrients. Older adults who take vitamin-mineral supplements show
               enhanced health and physical functioning, as indicated by several studies
               cited in the text. p. 568

17.10   A   Primary aging refers to genetically influenced declines that affect all
               members of our species and take place even in the context of overall good
               health. Secondary aging is due to hereditary defects and negative
               environmental influences, such as poor diet, lack of exercise, disease,
               substance abuse, environmental pollution, and psychological stress. p. 570

17.11   C   Unlike osteoarthritis, which is limited to certain joints, rheumatoid arthritis
               involves the whole body. An autoimmune response leads to inflammation
               of connective tissue, particularly the membranes that line the joints. p. 570

17.12   C   At age 65 and older, the death rate from unintentional injuries is at an all-
               time high. Motor vehicle collisions and falls are largely responsible. p. 571

17.13   C   Alzheimer's disease is the most common form of dementia, accounting for
               50 to 60 percent of all cases. p. 573

17.14   C   Inside neurons, neurofibrillary tangles appear—bundles of twisted threads
               that are the product of collapsed neural structures.   p. 573

17.15   B   Among people age 75 and older, Caucasian Americans are one-and-a-half
               times more likely to be institutionalized than are African Americans.
               Similarly, Asian Americans use nursing homes less often than do Caucasian
               Americans because of greater availability of family members to provide
               care—a factor that also accounts for low rates of nursing home placement in
               Japan. p. 578

17.16   A   Elders who sustain high levels of functioning engage in selective
               optimization with compensation. That is, they narrow their goals, *selecting*
               personally valued activities as a way of *optimizing* (or maximizing) returns
               from their diminishing energy. They also come up with new ways of
               compensating for losses. p. 579

17.17   B   Like implicit memory, language comprehension changes very little in late
               life as long as conversational partners do not speak very quickly. p. 582

17.18   C   The multiple cognitive personality traits that make up wisdom can be
               summed up as expertise in the fundamental pragmatics of life. p. 583

17.19   D   Terminal decline refers to a steady, marked decrease in cognitive
               functioning prior to death. p. 584

17.20   A   Much less is available for elders with little education and limited income.
        Community senior centers with inexpensive offerings related to everyday
        living attract more low-SES people than do programs such as Elderhostel. p.
        585

Chapter 18: Answers

18.1   A   The capacity to view one's life in the larger context of all humanity—as the chance combination of one person and one segment in history—contributes to the serenity and contentment that accompanies ego integrity. p. 592

18.2   B   The elderly must find a constructive way of facing the reality of death—through investing in a longer future than their own lifespan. Attaining ego transcendence requires a continuing effort to make life more secure, meaningful, and gratifying for those who will go on after one dies. p. 593

18.3   B   When asked, 30 percent of one sample of elders claimed that the best part of life was "right now"! Middle age also received high marks, whereas childhood and adolescence ranked as less satisfying. These findings clearly contradict the widespread belief that older adults wish to be young again. p. 594

18.4   C   Longitudinal research reveals that agreeableness and acceptance of change increase in late adulthood, while sociability dips slightly. p. 595

18.5   B   The few people who attain this stage form an enlarged vision of an all-inclusive human community. They act to bring it about by standing up against persecution and injustice and by promoting a common good that serves the needs of diverse groups. Great religious leaders, such as Mahatma Gandhi and Martin Luther King, Jr., illustrate conjunctive faith. p.598

18.6   B   Negative life changes in very old age are greater for women than for men. Women over age 75 are far less likely to be married, have lower incomes, and suffer from more illnesses—especially ones that restrict mobility. Furthermore, elderly women more often say that others depend on them for emotional support. Not surprisingly, women of very advanced age report a lower sense of psychological well-being than do men. p. 602

18.7   B   Ethnic minority elders do not readily accept formal agency services unless the services use culturally sensitive practices and are connected to a neighborhood organization such as the church. p. 602

18.8   B   According to this view (activity theory), arranging conditions that permit elders to remain engaged in roles and relationships is vital for life satisfaction. p. 603

18.9   C   Although their social networks are smaller, more older adults than younger adults are happy with their current number of friends. p. 604

18.10   D   Compared with older adults in urban areas, elders residing in quiet neighborhoods in small and mid-sized communities are more satisfied with life. The major reason is that smaller communities have lower crime rates. p. 606

18.11   D   Increasing numbers of ethnic minority elders want to live on their own, but poverty often prevents them from doing so. p. 607

18.12   B   The 5 percent of Americans age 65 and older who live in nursing homes experience the most extreme restriction of autonomy. p. 608

18.13   C   First, perceptions of fairness in the relationship increase as men participate more in household tasks after retirement. Second, with extra time together, the majority of couples engage in more joint leisure activities. Finally, greater emotional understanding and emphasis on regulating emotion in relationships lead to more positive interactions among older couples. p. 609

18.14   D   Elders have fewer lasting problems than do younger individuals, probably because death in later life is expected and viewed as less unfair. p. 610

18.15   B   Elderly women mention acceptance as a primary aspect of close friendship. Late-life friends shield one another from others' negative judgments about their capacities and worth as a person, which frequently stem from stereotypes of aging. p. 613

18.16   B   In interviews with a nationally representative sample, elders reported that exchanges of advice with adult children were most common. To avoid dependency, older parents expect more emotional support than practical assistance. p. 614

18.17   C   Many abusers are dependent, emotionally or financially, on their victims. This dependency, experienced as powerlessness, can lead to aggressive, exploitative behavior. p. 615

18.18   D   On the average, women tend to retire earlier than men, largely because family events—husband's retirement or the need to care for an ill spouse or parent—play larger roles in their decisions. p. 617

18.19   B   Younger, better educated, and financially secure elders with social interests
            are more likely to volunteer, and women do so more often than men.
            Nonvolunteers are especially receptive to volunteer activities in the first 2
            years after retiring—a prime time to recruit them into these personally
            rewarding and socially useful pursuits. p. 619

18.20   A   Recent definitions of successful aging have turned away from specific
            achievements toward processes people use to reach personally valued goals.
            p. 619

Chapter 19: Answers

19.1   C   Death is long and drawn out for three-fourths of people—many more than in times past—due to life-saving medical technology. p. 628

19.2   B   Clinical death is a short interval (following the agonal phase and preceding mortality) in which heartbeat, circulation, breathing, and brain functioning stop, but resuscitation is still possible. p. 629

19.3   B   Someone whose brain stem continues to function but whose cortex shows no electrical activity has entered a persistent vegetative state but is not brain dead. p. 629

19.4   D   Compared with earlier generations, today's children and adolescents in developed nations are insulated from death. Residents of inner-city ghettos, where violence is part of everyday existence, are exceptions. But overall, more young people reach adulthood without having experienced the death of someone they know well. This distance from death undoubtedly contributes to a sense of uneasiness about it. p. 630

19.5   C   Nonfunctionality is the most difficult component of the death concept for children to grasp. When they first comprehend nonfunctionality, they do so in terms of its most visible aspects, such as heartbeat and breathing. Only later do they understand that thinking, feeling, and dreaming cease. p. 631

19.6   A   Among Westerners, spirituality—a sense of life's meaning—is more important than religious commitment in reducing death anxiety. p. 634

19.7   B   Progress can be arrested at any stage, and some people move back and forth between stages. p. 635

19.8   D   A dying patient who has reached the stage of acceptance disengages from all but a few family members, friends, and caregivers. p. 636

19.9   D   According to recent theorists, a single strategy, such as acceptance, is not best for every dying patient. Instead, an appropriate death is a concept that makes sense in terms of the individual's pattern of living and values and, at the same time, preserves or restores significant relationships and is as free of suffering as possible. p. 636

19.10   C   A candid approach, in which everyone close to and caring for the dying person acknowledges the terminal illness, is best. Yet this also introduces the burden of participating in the work of dying with the patient—bringing relationships to closure, reflecting on life, and dealing with fears and regrets. Because some people find it hard to engage in these tasks, they pretend that the disease is not as bad as it is. p. 637

19.11   A   A strong sense of spirituality reduces fear of death. Informal reports from
              health professionals suggest that this is as true for dying patients as for
              people in general. p. 637

19.12   A   Passive euthanasia is an ordinary part of normal medical practice in which
              life-sustaining treatment is withheld or withdrawn, permitting a patient to
              die naturally. p. 640

19.13   A   People can best ensure that their wishes will be followed by preparing an
              advance medical directive—a written statement of desired medical
              treatment should they become incurably ill. Two types of advance directives
              are recognized in most states. p. 641

19.14   C   In gay and lesbian and other close relationships not sanctioned by law, the
              durable power of attorney can ensure the partner's role. p. 642

19.15   B   Central to the hospice approach is that the dying person and his or her
              family should be offered choices that guarantee an appropriate death. p. 639

19.16   B   We respond to loss with grief—intense physical and psychological distress.
              p. 645

19.17   A   Most of these responses are symptoms of depression—an invariable
              component of grieving. p. 646

19.18   D   As grief subsides in the accommodation phase, attention starts to shift to the
              surrounding world. p. 646

19.19   B   Regardless of children's level of understanding, honesty, affection, and
              reassurance help them tolerate painful feelings of loss. Keeping the truth
              from children isolates them and often leads to profound regrets. p. 647

19.20   D   Research reveals that using a lecture style leads to gains in knowledge but
              often leaves students more uncomfortable about death than they were
              before. In contrast, experiential programs that help people confront their
              own mortality are less likely to heighten death anxiety and sometimes
              reduce it. p. 650